THE MIGHTY ATOM

THE MIGHTY ATOM

The Life of Boxing Legend JIMMY WILDE

ADRIAN KNOTT

FOREWORD BY COLIN HART

pitch

First published by Pitch Publishing, 2024

Pitch Publishing
9 Donnington Park,
85 Birdham Road,
Chichester,
West Sussex,
PO20 7AJ
www.pitchpublishing.co.uk
info@pitchpublishing.co.uk

A CIP catalogue record is available for this book from the British Library.

ISBN 978 1 80150 905 3

Typesetting and origination by Pitch Publishing

Printed and bound by Thomson Press, India

CONTENTS

To the memory of

my mother

Gladys

and to those long forgotten

boxers from Wilde's era

who fought every week to

put food on the table.

FOREWORD

IN MY 60 years as a boxing writer I've had the good fortune and the privilege to have covered the careers of many of the greatest fighters who have graced the sport with their outstanding skills, power and courage.

I have been extremely lucky to have been ringside in an age that gave us so many fighters who are considered immortal: Muhammad Ali, Larry Holmes, Joe Frazier, George Foreman, Lennox Lewis, Mike Tyson, Sugar Ray Leonard, Marvelous Marvin Hagler, Roberto Duran, Thomas 'Hit Man' Hearns, Julio Cesar Chavez, Ken Buchanan, John Conteh and Joe Calzaghe are just a few.

Experiencing so much brilliance close-up should be enough to satisfy the most avid fan – who could possibly ask for more?

Yet if I had to choose one fighter I would love to have had the opportunity of watching from all those I didn't have the pleasure of seeing it wouldn't be Jack Dempsey, Joe Louis, Willie Pep, Sugar Ray Robinson or Henry Armstrong.

The one man whose CV has had me in awe ever since I began reading about boxing as a child was that freak of nature - Jimmy Wilde.

I always envied my father who as a 12-year-old on an August afternoon in 1918 was taken to see Jimmy headline a charity show at Chelsea's Stamford Bridge ground where he KO'd Joe Conn in the 12th round.

When the arguments start as to who pound-for-pound was the greatest British fighter of all time inevitably the wee Welshman gets the unanimous vote.

It beggars belief that a man who looked as if he was suffering from malnutrition – pale, painfully skinny with pipe-stem arms – was a ferocious punching wrecking machine.

Weighing 6st 10lb soaking wet and standing slightly more than 5ft 2in, such was his phenomenal concussive force he used to knock out 9st featherweights.

In twelve historic years from 1911–23 (he was world flyweight champion for seven of those years) Jimmy had 137 fights, scoring 99 knockouts and lost just four times.

When he started out as a pro after hundreds of fights in fairground boxing booths he went unbeaten in 103 contests – the greatest unbeaten run in history – a record that will never be broken.

America's *The Ring* magazine (considered boxing's bible) rated Wilde as the third greatest puncher of all time, the greatest flyweight ever and the 13th greatest fighter of the 20th Century.

Most fighters are fortunate if they are known worldwide by a nickname: The Greatest, Homicide Hank, Iron Mike and Hit Man are classic examples. Because of his dominance over his contemporaries, his blistering speed and the dynamite he carried in both fists, Jimmy was awarded three – The Mighty Atom, The Ghost With the Hammer in his Hand and The Tylorstown Terror.

So much has been written about him but none so eloquently or comprehensively than by Adrian Knott in this brilliantly researched biography – it is a thoroughly enjoyable read and for Adrian it was obviously a labour of love.

Unfortunately it had a sad ending with Jimmy poverty-stricken and spending the last four years of his life in hospital but The Mighty Atom had the satisfaction of knowing he was loved and admired far beyond the small mining village where he was born and grew up.

Colin Hart
Boxing Columnist
The Sun

ACKNOWLEDGEMENTS

FIRST AND foremost I would like to thank boxing historian Miles Templeton. Miles has spent the past 50-odd years scouring newspapers in libraries up and down the land collating results and information and now has a database that contains the records and fight reports of over 75,000 British boxers from 1890 to 1983. When I contacted Miles four years ago with the idea of writing this book he not only gave me great encouragement, he very kindly sent me reports of every one of Jimmy Wilde's fights which made my task a lot less daunting. I also thank him for his patience and willingness to help whenever I rang him up unannounced asking for extra information.

A special mention must also go to Hywel Matthews and Simon Golding, the archivists at Pontypridd Library, who were always on hand to provide me with any information that I requested.

I would like to thank the staff at the British Newspaper Archive for their magnificent online resource and to fellow author Lawrence Davies, who kindly shared with me his knowledge of Welsh mountain fighters one evening over the telephone.

Special thanks go to Colin Hart for agreeing to write a foreword. Colin is known and respected throughout the world as a top boxing journalist and I am honoured that he has contributed to the book.

I am also extremely grateful to all the staff at Pitch Publishing for their help and support.

INTRODUCTION

JIMMY WILDE was a boxing phenomenon. Just 5ft 2in in height, in his prime he never weighed more than 6st 10lb, yet he beat men who were often 2st heavier than himself. It is amazing to think that if he were boxing today, Jimmy would have been 11lb inside the strawweight limit of 7st 7lb, boxing's lightest weight class. Even so, if he had been fighting now he would, without doubt, have won world titles at strawweight, light-flyweight, flyweight and super-flyweight.

Born into a proud mining community in south Wales, Jimmy was working in the mines at just 11 years of age. He was taught to box by his workmate, a former bare-knuckle fighter named Dai Davies – a man who would eventually become Jimmy's father-in-law.

Many have wondered how such a tiny, frail-looking man could have such disproportionate knockout power. Davies taught Jimmy to throw a punch as his opponent was leaning in. It was a move that required expert timing, but it gave Jimmy's punches twice the force on impact.

As a fighter, Jimmy was one of the greatest in boxing history. He was the undefeated British and world flyweight champion from 1916–1923. One hundred years after his last fight, he is still considered the greatest flyweight of all time, even though he weighed 18lb *under* the 8st limit throughout the best years of his career.

When Jimmy fought, boxing was a different sport than it is today. In Jimmy's day, to win the British title you had to be the best fighter in the country. Not like nowadays where a fighter can win a Lonsdale belt and be ranked eighth or ninth in the domestic rankings. Back then, a British champion was a national hero.

Boxing has always been a tough, brutal, unforgiving sport. In Wilde's day, it was even more so. Every village and town had its share of decent boxers. Most of these young lads fought ten-rounders every week for small purses. There was no regulatory body to oversee the sport, so they could fight as often as they wished. Most of them were too brave for their own good and took beating after beating. The unlucky ones got brain damage by their mid-30s. Some went blind.

Boxers wore 4oz gloves filled with horsehair and few fighters wore gum shields. Training camps did not exist; fighters kept fit by fighting. There was no such thing as a promotional contract. A boxer was free to fight whoever he liked. There were no rankings, so fighters fought often and had to build a reputation by beating other good fighters. Boxers were tough, but they were exemplary sportsmen. Challenges would be issued by a fighter's manager, who would advertise his wish for his boy to box in papers like *Boxing* and *Mirror of Life*. All far removed from today, when fighters throw insults or pretend to hate each other in order to drum up interest.

In the ring, Jimmy was a master of controlling a fight. He would stand with his hands by his waist and dart in and out with fast jabs and hard right crosses. He could fight on the offensive or counter-punch. The old boxing adage 'make him miss, make him pay' is a perfect description of how Wilde fought. On the rare occasions he did get caught, he showed he had a great chin and, like all great champions, he was most dangerous when he had just been hurt. He could change the way a fight was going with one punch and he would never let his man off the hook once he had him in trouble.

Jimmy Wilde was not only a great boxer, he was a superstar of his era long before the age of instant celebrity. He was a close friend of the Prince of Wales, Prince William of Sweden and Lord Lonsdale. He endorsed Epsom salts, boxing equipment, malt drinks and raised thousands of pounds during the First World War by fighting in exhibitions. He was as much at ease in the company of royalty as he was having a game of snooker at the miners' welfare club back home in Tylorstown.

While researching and writing this book, I was pleased to find that, during his life, Jimmy was admired and respected as much out of the ring as he was in it. Nevertheless, today he is remembered by only the most ardent of boxing fans. I hope this book keeps the memory of a true boxing legend well and truly alive.

Adrian Knott
November 2023

1

A Hungry Childhood

ONE MORNING in 1872, a group of well-dressed men got off a train at Quakers Yard, a sparsely populated hamlet six miles north of Pontypridd, deep in the Welsh valleys. Although the men were from London, they knew the exact place where they were going. They walked roughly one mile to a vast area of empty farmland.

Well over 3,000 acres of lush green land, which had the Taff Bargoed river running through it, stretched out in front of them. The men pointed in all directions, looked all around them and nodded in agreement before making their way back to the station.

One of the men who had visited that day was London businessman F.W. Harris. He had seen the potential to mine coal in the area and, in the autumn of 1872, he purchased the farmland and set to work on building a colliery.

Over the next four years, hundreds of men were employed to fell trees, dig shafts and put in place the two huge winding machines. The two shafts were 180ft apart and nearly 800 yards deep, making what would become known as Harris's Deep Navigation Colliery the deepest in south Wales at that time. Like many who had set up mines in the vicinity, Harris named this new burgeoning community after himself. Harristown was born, although the locals preferred to use the Welsh translation of Treharris.

Within a decade, an uninhabited rural idyll had been transformed into a thriving town of just over 4,000 people. Men from all parts of south Wales and as far afield as Shropshire came to Treharris, either alone or with their families, in search of work.

One of these men was James Wilde. Born in 1867 in the nearby hamlet of Llanfabon, James Wilde had been a colliery labourer all his life. At the age of 23, he married a 19-year-old local woman named Margaret Evans in Newtown, Pontypridd. Within a year, they had settled in Treharris and had their first child, a daughter, Mary Anne.

For every family living in a mining town, life was unrelentingly hard, especially during the long, dark winter months. Many pit workers only saw daylight on Sundays, when they were not at work. Toiling underground was physically back-breaking, as well as being dangerous. Profit was all that really mattered to the mine owners who saw the workforce as easily replaceable. Every day, the men had to deal with the threat of flash floods, roof collapses, runaway coal wagons potentially crushing them and the fear of dying from the silent killer – carbon monoxide poisoning. The most common and unavoidable danger was pneumoconiosis. This developed in the lungs through breathing in tiny particles of coal dust. It was a condition that was debilitating and, ultimately, fatal.

The Wildes lived at 28 Webster Street, which was adjacent to Harris's colliery. James Wilde was an underground horse driver.

Also living in the same house was one James Thomas (who worked as a colliery timber man) and his wife, as well as their four young children. Living in such overcrowded conditions with next to no privacy was common at this time. The 1891 census states that there were 524 people living in 82 dwellings in Webster Street alone.

Typical of all couples at that time, James and Margaret were intent on raising a large family, despite the economic hardships they faced on a daily basis. Their second child would go on to be the most well known. James Edward Wilde was born on 12 May 1892 in a small chapel in nearby Quakers Yard. Three more children would follow: Catherine in 1896, Ellen Jane in 1899 and Elias in 1901.[1]

In his autobiography, *Fighting Was My Business*, Jimmy would write of how the one over-riding and ever-present feeling he had when he was a small boy was that of hunger. 'There were times, particularly during the strikes, when starvation was not far away.'[2]

It wasn't only strikes in the mines that colliers had to worry about. A rail strike could be equally detrimental. No working railway meant the mine would have to close and the workers would be reliant on paltry relief payments which could not sustain a family for any length of time.

Despite its massive output of high quality coal, Harris's colliery was not immune to strikes and other disputes which culminated in workers being laid off without notice. Both scenarios were economically crippling for families. During these

1 Most sources wrongly give Wilde's date of birth as 15 May 1892

2 Jimmy Wilde *Fighting Was My Business* p.11

periods of unemployment, many families found themselves close to starvation. The Quakers would help by setting up makeshift soup kitchens at the end of the street and the Salvation Army brass band would march through the rows of terraced houses playing their instruments, hoping that the better-off would make a donation. Many fit and healthy men and women visibly lost weight during these desperate times. Some succumbed to illness and died.

It is difficult to know exactly when James and Margaret Wilde moved their young family out of Treharris. But move they did, roughly nine miles west, to Tylorstown in the Ferndale valley.

Tylorstown (just has Treharris had been) was an isolated area of farmland until Alfred Tylor made his way from London and purchased Pendyrus Farm in the early 1870s. Tylor built a colliery there and, with it, a new community. Long rows of small terraced houses were built, woven into the valleys, and this new town was named after the man who had formed it.

By the time James Wilde and his young family moved to Tylorstown, Pendyrus colliery was producing nearly 250,000 tonnes of coal per year. Between 1891 and 1901, the population of Tylorstown tripled to just over 3,000. This is where James Wilde would settle for the rest of his life. His son, through his deeds in the boxing ring, would make this small town in the Rhondda valley known throughout the world.

The 1901 census tells us that Jimmy's new home was a small terraced house at 8 Station Road. The houses were 'all alike to look at, all covered with the grime of the Rhondda valley'.[3]

3 Jimmy Wilde *Fighting Was My Business* p.12

Young Jimmy's earliest memories are that of his father returning home from working at the pit, his face black with coal dust, which accentuated the whiteness of his eyes. His father would wash off the dust and dirt in a tin bath placed in front of the open fire in their tiny living room. Margaret would always make sure her husband had a newly washed and ironed shirt to wear. To help pay the rent, many families took in a lodger (normally a fellow collier) who had recently arrived in the area. The Wildes were no exception.

The street outside his house was where young Jimmy, like all children, spent most of his time. He would play hopscotch and tick, skipping and jostling with the other boys and girls. Tylorstown, like all pit villages in south Wales, was a tough, uncompromising place. Money was in short supply and little affection was shown to children by their parents. They were counting down the days to when their offspring could start bringing in a wage.

Jimmy's small stature was the main reason he got into so many playground scraps when he was young. Bigger boys saw him as an easy target at first. What they didn't know was that Jimmy actually enjoyed the rough and tumble of combat. Although he seemed 'stunted and undernourished',[4] Jimmy's frail physique helped him evade the blows and kicks that came his way. When he retaliated with fast – albeit light – blows, it caused his bigger assailants a great deal of frustration.

Tylorstown was just as deprived as Treharris had been and the threat of strikes was never far away. Nevertheless, Jimmy had a

4 Jimmy Wilde *Fighting Was My Business* p.12

cheerful attitude. Sometimes this was misconstrued as insolence, especially when he was at school and being disciplined for unruly behaviour or poor time-keeping. Being physically punished by a teacher never seemed to bother him or break his spirit.

Jimmy hated school and would do anything possible to avoid going. In a way, his family's economic hardship gave him a handy excuse for playing truant. Being out of school meant he and his eldest sister could find ways of supplementing the meagre family coffers.

One of the ways in which Jimmy and his sister, Mary Anne, raised some money came about purely by chance. One morning, Jimmy saw a gang of older lads carrying heavy sacks. Jimmy followed them at a safe distance and watched the boys as they carefully hid the sacks. Jimmy rushed home to tell his sister. They both went back to investigate. Jimmy and Mary Anne were expecting the sacks to be stuffed with rabbits, but they were filled to the brim with coal.

The following morning, Jimmy went to check on the sacks. They had gone. The three boys were caned for being late for school. Jimmy knew that they had spent the morning selling coal. The only problem Jimmy had was that he did not know where they had got the coal from. For the next four mornings, Jimmy woke at dawn and went looking for the boys. There was no sign of them. On the fifth morning, the boys went past his house and Jimmy and Mary Anne followed them to a coal tip. The tip was five miles from Station Road, but somehow Jimmy, all 4st of him, and his sister filled a sack they had brought with them with three-quarters of a hundredweight of coal when the boys had gone and 'were in a state of collapse when we eventually reached Tylorstown'.[5] Jimmy and Mary Anne got one shilling and nine pence when they sold the coal later that day.

Stealing and selling coal was born out of necessity for Jimmy and his sister. They soon realised that a ten-mile round trip was too much, so they tried their luck closer to home. This time it did not work out so well.

Early one morning, after filling up a sack, they were spotted as they crossed the railway track and Jimmy and Mary Anne only got away because their pursuer stumbled and fell. From now on, Mary Anne reasoned, they would never raid a coal tip fewer than five miles from home for fear of being recognised. That being said, sometimes a local pit man, sympathetic to the way things were, would turn a blind eye to Jimmy and Mary Anne or warn them of impending danger so that they had ample time to get away without being chased. Jimmy and Mary Anne did this for nearly a year until four local boys were arrested by the local constabulary. From now on, Jimmy and Mary Anne agreed, a safer way of making money would have to be devised.

During the summer months, Jimmy and his sister would rise at dawn and walk up to seven miles through the valleys to pick blackberries which they would later sell to their neighbours and people in the adjoining streets. If there was a strike and they had already sold all the blackberries, Jimmy and Mary Anne would make beer with dandelions and sell that instead. All of these money-

5 Jimmy Wilde *Fighting Was My Business* p.15

making ventures meant that Jimmy was invariably late for school. Many times he was reprimanded. But money had to be made.

Young Jimmy was still fighting in the playground, but it was in the street that fights had a little more riding on them; namely a packet of cigarettes, which cost one penny. These would be sold to the pit men. Boys would gather and form a ring around the two lads who were fighting and battle would commence. Because he was so tiny, Jimmy never had any backers, unlike the other boys. Nevertheless, he had a great ability to dodge and slip blows and then give some back. His slender frame belied a wiry toughness and invariably he would be the last one standing.

The boys Jimmy fought in the street were always heavier than him, but they would tire themselves out trying to hit him. Jimmy would then wade into them with blurring hand speed. The more fights Jimmy had, the more his exploits and fistic notoriety spread among his peers. 'I think my mother and father lived in fear of my getting into serious trouble,' he would later write.[6]

Although he enjoyed fighting, Jimmy did not have a boxing hero at this time, but he had seen boxing at the annual local fair. This aroused his interest in the noble art and he began reading boxing books, which he borrowed from the library. The playground scraps were the same sort of set-tos every boy all over the country had, but boxing was slowly becoming of more interest to him.

Jimmy would spend many an hour listening with great interest to an uncle or a grandfather of one of his school pals, who would

6 Jimmy Wilde *Fighting Was My Business* p.21

tell exciting tales of old Welsh bare-knuckle fighters who had become legends in the particular hamlet or village they had lived in. Scrapping, whether it be in the playground or in the street, was exciting – not to mention a way of earning money. What is more, it took Jimmy's mind off the day when he would have to leave school and work in the mines. The thought filled Jimmy with dread. 'One day school, the next day the pit head and the dreaded cage.'[7]

Jimmy's anxiety about going down the mines was exacerbated by the fact there were problems at home. His father's health was deteriorating, which meant he could not work. Living on Poor Relief and having to queue with the other poor souls coughing their lungs up as they waited to collect their money from the Board of Guardians at the local parish office was a strain, both physically and mentally. It was a severe blow to a man's pride to stand and wait for his name to be called out, but it had to be done. Pride alone would not put food on the table.

The lack of money coming in caused endless arguments between James and Margaret. She started to spend less time at the family home in Station Road and would often take the youngest children with her to stay with friends nearby.

7 Jimmy Wilde *Fighting Was My Business* p.24

2

Meeting Dai Davies

JIMMY WAS just 11 when he went to work in the pit. He stood a few inches under four and a half feet and weighed less than 5st. Wearing heavy boots and hand-me-down pit clothes, he made his way to the colliery filled with fear and trepidation. Jimmy was assigned to number eight pit at Ferndale colliery. He dutifully reported to the clerk, who introduced him to his new workmates. Little did Jimmy know that day that he would later meet the man who would not only teach him the rudiments of boxing but also become his father-in-law.

Ferndale colliery consisted of nine pit heads that were all within a one-mile radius of one another. Nearly 14,000 men were employed there when Jimmy started work.

In his autobiography, Jimmy vividly recalled the first time he went down the pit: 'I remember the call of "hold tight", the gate closing and then the descent. Slow at first, then bewilderingly fast. Daylight disappeared like a quick dusk. Soon the blackness was only broken by a few safety lamps which seemed to spread no effective light.'[8] At just over 600 yards in depth, pit number eight was the deepest in the Rhondda.

It took only one minute for the cage lift to reach the bottom of the shaft. An old hand advised Jimmy to stand still for a moment so that his eyes could get accustomed to the darkness. When Jimmy's eyes did adjust, he was able to make out the trams on the rails in the distance, the faint light emanating from the lamps and the deep black, wet walls. There is no doubt that the men who Jimmy was working with were a tough breed, but they were decent upstanding men all the same. 'There was a bluff heartiness about the miners. Little sympathy was wasted on youngsters down there for the first time, but there was a genuine kindness to them.'[9]

Because he was so small, Jimmy was given the task of watering coal dust and watching the coal trucks as they came past on the rails, each one filled with up to a tonne of coal. Jimmy had to record how many trucks had gone past and check they were all full. His first few weeks underground were exhausting. Any thoughts of boxing were well and truly put to the back of his mind. After a 12-hour shift in the mines, having a hot meal and getting off to bed was all Jimmy was fit for.

Slowly but surely, Jimmy got used to the lift cage, the sudden darkness, the noise and the speed of the rail trams. He also got used to the coarse jokes and the harsh language of his fellow workers. He soon found out that most, if not all, miners had a love of fist fighting. It was a noble way to settle a dispute and, in the mines, there were plenty of those. Petty squabbles would

8 Jimmy Wilde *Fighting Was My Business* p.26
9 Jimmy Wilde *Fighting Was My Business* p.27

often quickly get out of hand and were nearly always settled by fisticuffs.

A neutral man would be on hand to ensure there was no kneeing, kicking, biting or gouging and the fights would be over in a matter of seconds. When inching himself sideways into a crevice that bigger men found impossible to get into in order to hew the coal, Jimmy would listen to the stories the miners told; who they had seen fight or how they themselves had taken part in a fight in the hills and earned some extra money for their family.

Bare-knuckle fighting was strictly illegal, so the men and their backers would trek over the mountains until they had found a secluded spot which was far enough away from prying eyes and detection by the police. Each fighter had a 'second' in his corner and a referee would be appointed to keep order. There were no ropes. Instead, the fighters would be encircled by the crowd, who were there not only to watch the fight, but to bet on it. These fights were brutal affairs. Because the fighters did not wear gloves, bad cuts and lacerations were common. A man's face could swell quickly and a well-placed punch around the eye socket could close a man's eye shut within seconds. Despite these injuries, most fighters carried on until they were too exhausted to continue and it was only then that the fight would be deemed to be over.

Some men fought 'in the holes'. This was a particularly barbaric activity. A hole would be dug on a flat piece of land, normally to waist height. Two men would then jump into the hole and fight in there until one of them was either knocked out or too badly injured to carry on.

Dai Davies was one of these mountain fighters. Born in 1873 in Monmouthshire, he had worked as a haulier in the mines since he was a small boy. He had also had hundreds of bare-knuckle fights. A stocky man, his shoulders were rounded and hard with muscle. His hands were big for a man of his size and his huge calloused knuckles betrayed what he did in his spare time. His face bore testimony to hard fistic battles. He had heavy scar tissue above both eyebrows and, although he had high cheekbones, normally such a hindrance to a fighter, he carried no other facial scars.

Dai was lucky. He had the sense to give up fighting before his brain became scrambled from taking too many punches. In every pub in every village in south Wales, an ex-mountain fighter who was old before his time could be found, their faculties shot to pieces by the wear and tear of their former trade.

Whether it was fate that brought Jimmy and Dai together will never be known. What is certain is that, when Jimmy started working with Dai in the mines, he found not only someone who knew about fighting, he found a man who could put him at ease and instil confidence in him. Dai was a second father to Jimmy. Strong physically and mentally, Dai was a quiet man who exuded self-belief without needing to show off or boast.

At first, Jimmy was reluctant to ask Dai about his fighting past. He need not have worried. Dai was only too pleased to tell him stories in between knocking out chunks of coal with his pick axe, while Jimmy picked them up and placed them in the nearby coal truck.

One day, Dai asked Jimmy if he had any intention of fighting seriously. Jimmy responded in the affirmative, but he was worried about his size, or lack of it. Dai, however, was undeterred. In fact, Dai had already heard about Jimmy's street fights against boys who were a stone or two heavier, of how he had been able to take everything they had thrown at him and still been the last one standing. He told Jimmy: 'One day I'll see you fight. We might be able to make something out of you.'[10]

Until that time, Jimmy would take instruction from Dai when they were having a break. Dai would stand in front of Jimmy and teach him how to slip a punch, how to block and parry, how to clinch effectively. With such limited space, movement was restricted, so Dai encouraged Jimmy to sway away from punches, all the time telling Jimmy that nothing tired an opponent faster than repeatedly being made to miss.

Jimmy was now spending more and more time with Dai. Many nights after work, he would go to Dai's house and carry on with the boxing lessons in the tiny bedroom upstairs. Learning to box in such a small room had its advantages, the main one being that it allowed little room for manoeuvre. As Dai threw punches, Jimmy would be forced to block them on his forearms or parry the blows with his right hand. With no space in which to move around, Jimmy was forced to master the art of slipping punches or ducking them. He would then quickly step to the

10 Jimmy Wilde *Fighting Was My Business* p.32

side and throw a counter-punch. Throughout his career, Jimmy never skirted around the ring wasting energy. It was all about economy of movement. This is one of the main reasons he was able to knock out bigger men. He forced them to exert themselves and, by deftly making them miss, he would know when they were starting to wilt and when they were ready to be taken out.

Dai's wife, Sarah, had always been totally opposed to fighting in any form, but she had learned to tolerate it where Dai was concerned. She had quickly come to the conclusion that it was pointless trying to stop her husband. When they were younger, she had told anyone who would listen that the only thing that would stop him would be Father Time. Although Sarah was uneasy about Dai encouraging little Jimmy to fight, she was always on hand with a cup of tea for them both when they had finished. As well as the boxing lessons, Jimmy had another reason to keep popping round to the Davies's house.

Their daughter, Elizabeth, who was two years younger than Jimmy, had caught his eye. Jimmy, however, was too shy to properly speak to her. Elizabeth was an apprentice dressmaker and, at first, Jimmy was worried he was too unrefined for her. Jimmy tried many times to strike up a conversation with Elizabeth but, frustratingly, he would be met with short replies. This did nothing to alleviate Jimmy's feelings of insecurity about the possibility of them becoming a couple. As time passed, though, Elizabeth slowly started to take more notice of him. Little did Jimmy know that she felt the same for him as he did for her.

Dai eventually got his wish to see Jimmy in action. One day down in the mine, Jimmy and another boy named Tommy Davies (who had experience of fighting in a boxing booth) got into an altercation. Tempers flared and, before they knew it, the boys were encircled by men urging them to fight. Tommy Davies was a good 3st heavier than Jimmy and lunged at him with fury. Jimmy kept sidestepping. Ducking. Weaving. The enraged and frustrated Davies launched himself at Jimmy in one last big effort to put Jimmy away. Jimmy, though, had anticipated the move. He planted his feet and waited for Davies to throw a punch. Jimmy made Davies miss. Davies was wide open for a smashing right cross that Jimmy landed on the side of the boy's jaw. Down Davies went. Flat on his back in the coal dust. A fellow miner counted to ten and then started to revive him. Dai stood there watching. He couldn't put his finger on it exactly, but he knew that Jimmy had that special 'something' that all champions have.

After Jimmy's showing against Tommy Davies, Dai now had serious intentions of taking him to fight on a boxing booth, but their plans were to be cruelly interrupted.

One day at the colliery, Jimmy was given a new job above ground. As the coal trams travelled up the sidings, Jimmy had to grease the metal pulleys. He was doing this one day when all of a sudden he was knocked flat on his back and dragged across the ground by the metal pulley which had become embedded in his right calf. The pulley had cut through the muscle and gone through to the bone. The pulley eventually worked free and Jimmy, who was in absolute agony, crawled on his chest a short distance to safety. A short time later, someone found him lying in the mud semi-conscious. His lower leg was covered in blood. A couple of miners patched him up best as they could and took him home.

Home for Jimmy was now with Dai, Sarah and Elizabeth at 49 Brondeg Street. The situation at Station Road between Jimmy's mother and father had become strained. With Jimmy's strong friendship with Dai, it had been decided that it would be best for all concerned for Jimmy to move in with them.

Jimmy's leg was in a bad way, according to Doctor Morris. He told Jimmy that it would be at last three months before he would be back on his feet. Three months seemed like an eternity. It wasn't all bad, though, once he got used to it. He spent a lot of time in bed reading boxing books and, more importantly, Elizabeth's icy disposition towards him had thawed.

Jimmy's leg did indeed take three months to heal. After that, he had to spend a further couple of months hobbling around on crutches before his leg was strong enough for him to return to work.

3

Boxing Booth Fighter

'GENTLEMEN! GENTLEMEN! Here we have the finest ring men in all of Wales. You sir! You look like you can handle yerself. Do yer fancy having a go? One pound is yours if you can last three rounds with one of our fantastic fighters here.'

This is what the owner of the fairground boxing booth would shout out to the crowd while pointing at his troupe of boxers, who were standing on the stage in their satin and velvet boxing robes. It would not be long before a fellow in the crowd (who'd had a few too many pints of beer and some hearty encouragement from his mates) would accept the challenge. A tatty pair of gloves would be thrown down to him and up the steps he would clamber, on to the stage, past the fighters and into the marquee tent behind the gaudy façade of the booth. Once in the marquee, he would climb into the ring, where he would swiftly be parted from his senses. Laid out on the blood-stained canvas or, as was most often the case, simply beaten by exhaustion. This was Jack Scarrott's Boxing Pavilion.

John (Jack) Scarrott was born in 1870 in Newport and had been a decent fighter himself on the boxing booths. A tall, slim man with a thick moustache and a booming voice, the cane-carrying Scarrott was a showman through and through. Shortly after getting married at the age of 20, he decided, with much encouragement from his wife Priscilla, to finish with fighting and stay on the safe side of the ropes. Priscilla convinced him that owning a boxing booth was far more lucrative, and safer, than fighting in one, so Scarrott decided to set up his own in Pontypridd. By the time Jimmy Wilde was 15, Scarrott's had become the most popular touring booth in south Wales.

Life on the boxing booth was not for the faint-hearted. It was rough, unregulated and dangerous. There were certainly no ringside doctors. If a challenger from the crowd was knocked out, a bucket of cold water would be thrown over him to bring him round and he would be sent on his way.

Most of the men who worked on the fairground booths were retired bare-knuckle fighters who were still a bit useful and were looking to earn a few extra quid. Many of them did it simply because they missed having a fight and the little bit of adulation that came with it.

On the whole though, fairground booths featured mostly professional boxers who would now be classed as 'area level' fighters. They were tough and capable, but not quite good enough to be British champions. There were a few, like Jimmy, who hoped it would be a stepping stone to greater glories. For a young boxer, there was no better way to learn the trade. Despite it being a hard way of life (many fighters slept under the ring at night) working on the booths fostered a strong sense of camaraderie that the booth boxers cherished for the rest of their lives.

All boxing booths were run along the same lines. The owner would have his own group of boxers and the name of the game was to create a bit of theatre, drum up a crowd and make money. Booth fighters had to be able to do two things to be successful; they had to be a good boxer *and* a good actor.

The pro fighters on the booths seldom lost to the man off the street, but taking on all-comers required a lot of concentration nonetheless. Ex-mountain fighters from another town who wanted to prove a point, brawny farm labourers, fellows with next-to-no experience who were up for a fight after too much ale, youths who were out to impress a girl. They all had to be faced in the ring.

The owners of the fairground booths were, first and foremost, astute businessmen. A 'plant' would always be in the crowd just in case business was slow and there were no takers. If no volunteers were forthcoming, the 'plant' would raise his hand and accept the challenge. This type of fight was called a 'gee'. This meant the two pro fighters would go through the motions and make it look good. They were skilled and experienced enough to make it seem as if they were fighting for real when, in fact, they were pulling their punches. Hitting arms and elbows. One trick was to slap with an open glove. This did no damage whatsoever, but it sounded like a good punch had landed to those who were standing a few rows back.

Sometimes the 'plant' would be from another booth. The owner, having great knowledge of the fight scene, would often recognise him and ask him if he wanted a 'gee' or a straight fight. A straight fight was rarely chosen; it was hard enough having to fight all and sundry. On the few occasions when they did have a straight fight, and it had been a particularly entertaining one, 'nobbins' (coins that were thrown into the ring from an appreciative crowd) would be split between the two boxers at the end of the fight.

Jimmy Wilde was 15 when he went to see if he could secure a fight at Scarrott's booth. The experience was a little off-putting to say the least. Scarrott eyed Jimmy up and down and told him he was far too small. Scarrott did have a job for him, though – standin guard behind the tent making sure that nobody climbed in under the marquee canvas without paying.

Legend has it that one day Scarrott saw Jimmy fighting a group of youths who were trying to get in for free. The boys were all much bigger than Jimmy and the story goes that it was after seeing Jimmy knock them all out with ease that Scarrott decided he would be better off fighting for the booth rather than guarding it.

Boxing is full of mythical stories, but this one does seem plausible. There is no way Jimmy would have been taken on at the booth simply by presenting himself to Scarrott and offering to fight for him. He was too small and was unknown. Scarrott was a hard man who showed no sentiment. He would never have risked his reputation and livelihood by taking on someone he did not know about. Seeing Jimmy knock out bigger, older boys would undoubtedly have changed his mind.

At first, Scarrott had to put up with loud protests from the crowd when Jimmy was first seen in action at the booth. One night at Taffs Well in Pentyrch, a fellow who weighed in the region of 12st climbed into the ring with Jimmy. Howls of derision came from the crowd. Calls to 'stop it' were aimed at Scarrott, as well as shouts of 'you should be ashamed'. The crowd need not have worried. Scarrott reassured them that there was no need to be concerned for the lad's safety and that he was more than capable of looking after himself.

Scarrott's words proved prophetic. After a fairly quiet first round, Jimmy caught the bigger man with a perfectly timed right in the second. It took nearly ten minutes for his stricken opponent to come round.

Because of his small stature, many of the men in the crowd saw Jimmy as an easy fight. They soon learned the hard way that Jimmy had a cast iron temperament to go with his excellent ring generalship.

Most of the men who climbed into the ring at a travelling booth, to their own detriment, greatly underestimated the abilities of the professional boxers, especially if they had been drinking. As Jimmy wrote in his autobiography: 'Against these crude fighters, a knockout was coming as a matter of course.'[11]

Some of Jimmy's happiest times were on the road touring south Wales during the summer months. One time, they stopped

11 Jimmy Wilde *Fighting Was My Business* p.48

at Caerphilly. A mountain fighter fancied his chances and was insulted when Jimmy climbed into the ring. Sensing the brute's indignation, Scarrott offered him one pound for every *minute* that he lasted. This made the man even more irate. The gong sounded for the first bell, Jimmy hit him with two left hooks and the fight was over within five seconds. The mountain fighter got nothing except a headache. Jimmy was paid his usual five shillings.

Word had got around Caerphilly about Wilde. The following night, two big chaps walked up to Scarrott. They wanted to know more about the little lad who was laying out all and sundry. They thought it was a hoax, a big fix to drum up business. Scarrott wasn't fazed. He told the two men that, if they lasted four rounds between them, he would pay them a pound each.

Jimmy carried the first man in the first round for the benefit of the crowd and stopped him in the second. His friend was not so fortunate. He lasted a little over five seconds.

The fairground boxing booth was unlicensed boxing on magic mushrooms. There was always plenty of testosterone flying about and many times there would be crowd disorder. An innocent push or shove would often quickly escalate into a full-scale riot.

The booth did have its lighter moments. Sometimes these could border on the farcical. One night, a man who weighed at least 13st tried his luck with Jimmy (who weighed around 6st at this time). The fight was over within a minute and when the man came round, he did not even realise that he had been knocked out. He was so baffled that he argued with Scarrott in disbelief. Scarrott told the man that he had indeed been knocked out by the wisp of a boy in the opposite corner. The man rose to his feet, took a deep breath and launched himself across the ring towards Jimmy, who deftly stepped to one side. The enraged slugger's momentum propelled him head-first through the ropes and on to the floor, much to the delight of the raucous crowd.

It is impossible to know how many fights Wilde had at Scarrott's pavilion. They weren't recorded and nobody kept count. What is certain is that Jimmy's time on the booth had been a fistic education like no other and he held Scarrott in the highest regard for the rest of his life. 'Scarrott, in those early days, helped to make me, as he had helped to make many other champions.'[12]

Boxing on the booth had not only helped Wilde hone his craft, it had also provided him with much-needed extra money. He was still working 12-hour shifts at the colliery. The wages from the booth were a welcome boost and they had convinced Elizabeth that Jimmy had a future in boxing.

Jimmy was happy and content living with the Davies family at Brondeg Street, even though it was a little cramped – Dai and Sarah had eight children.

On 8 November 1910, Jimmy and Elizabeth were married at Pontypridd registry office. Thirty-five days later, their son, David, was born.

---

12 Jimmy Wilde *Fighting Was My Business* p.52

4
Steady Progress

AT THE beginning of 1911, Wilde was an 18-year-old husband and father. After his time on the booths, he was more determined than ever to make boxing his living so that he could leave the mines for good.

What was more important to Jimmy was that he now knew that he had the full backing of his wife. Elizabeth had initially been totally opposed to Jimmy fighting, but now she was fully behind him.

Elizabeth's support for Jimmy cannot be overstated. She was the driving force behind his success and was always there to reassure him, advise him and, when his career had progressed, keep his feet on the ground. Throughout his career, Elizabeth was never far from Jimmy's side and was an all-important extra pair of eyes and ears for him. Elizabeth was always on hand to help Jimmy sort out the good advice from the bad; who to trust and who to steer clear of. She was the epitome of domestic stability.

Jimmy was keen to maintain the momentum that he had built up at Scarrott's pavilion. After a discussion with Dai and

Elizabeth, they both came to the conclusion that he ought to go down to Pontypridd to see if any of the managers or promoters there would take him on.

Thomas Edward Lewis (known to all as 'Teddy') was born in 1863 in Llantwit Fardre, a few miles south of Pontypridd. When Teddy was a small boy, his father purchased a shoe shop in Pontypridd and the family moved there. The Lewis family never struggled financially and Teddy went on to be educated at Clifton College in Bristol, where his love of all sports flourished. He was an excellent swimmer in his youth, but sports administration was his true calling. He became the secretary of an athletics syndicate which went on to purchase Taff Vale Park and he helped set up the Welsh Powderhall sprint race which, at that time, was one of the biggest events in the Welsh sporting calendar.

The Powderhall Sprint was a 140-yard dash. During its peak years, crowds of more than 40,000 people would descend on Taff Vale Park to watch professional sprinters who came from all over the British Isles to compete. Teddy was the official starter for the race, as well as for the South Wales Athletics Board for more than two decades. Firing his starting pistol into the air thousands of times undoubtedly contributed to the deafness he suffered in his right ear. Rugby union was his other great interest and Teddy was the president of Pontypridd Rugby Football Club when he first met Jimmy. Like most Welshmen, Teddy also loved boxing. He set up the Millfield Boxing Club above the Millfield Hotel in the centre of Pontypridd where, once a week, he would stage boxing shows.

One Saturday, Wilde walked down to Pontypridd and strode up to the entrance of the Millfield Hotel. He told the two door attendants that he was here to secure a fight. They looked at Jimmy with smiles on their faces. They clearly did not believe him. Jimmy demanded to see the manager. Eventually, one of the attendants went upstairs and Teddy Lewis came down. Jimmy introduced himself to the short, grey-haired Lewis and his attitude was, thankfully, more accommodating than the door attendants'.

Lewis had seen many young fighters come and go in his time and he was a shrewd judge of character. He told Jimmy that he would have trouble matching him because of his small stature and that he would be better off going home and waiting until he had filled out a bit. Jimmy, to his credit, persisted. He told Lewis that, despite his lack of height and weight, he had never been beaten during his time fighting on Scarrott's booth.

Jimmy's pleading must have impressed Lewis. A boy who weighed six-stone-nothing and stood just over 5ft tall had made the effort to come down to Pontypridd looking for a fight. Although he did not show it, Lewis was impressed by that alone. Teddy sighed and told Jimmy that he would try his best to find an opponent for him and that he should come back the following Saturday.

Lewis was true to his word. He had found an opponent for Jimmy. The fight would only be an exhibition, but Jimmy did not mind. When he went up the stairs, Jimmy was led into a dimly lit, smoke-filled room in which a small boxing ring was surrounded by a hundred or so miners who were watching the fights.

Just like when he had started on Scarrott's booth, Wilde was met with derisory laughs when he first climbed into the ring at the Millfield. He looked so frail that many at ringside questioned Lewis's judgement, as well as his sanity. They changed their minds once they saw Wilde in action. They soon came to appreciate the skill of the little lad in the ring as he made lightweights and welterweights miss by a hair's breadth. Every Saturday afternoon, Wilde would race down to Pontypridd from Tylorstown to appear at the Millfield. For these exhibitions, Lewis paid Jimmy five shillings.

Wilde's name first appeared in print in boxing's trade paper on 25 February 1911. The previous week he had fought an exhibition against George Lake, an experienced lightweight from Cardiff. *Boxing* reported how Wilde had 'put up a very pretty six rounds of the exhibition order against George Lake who had a big pull in weight but dealt very kindly with the little lad'.

It is not known how many of these exhibitions Wilde took part in at the Millfield Athletic Club during 1911. Not every boxing show was reported on at the time due to the fact that there were so many of them. At the very least, he would have had one a week. Sometimes two. It is not inconceivable to think that Wilde could well have fought 100 exhibition bouts during that one year alone.

Throughout his time in sports administration and officiating, Teddy Lewis had always placed great importance on fairness. It is a measure of the man that he was willing to exercise such caution with Wilde in those early days. Wilde was always going to be conceding height, weight and reach to the man in the opposite corner, but Lewis was willing to invest the necessary time in him to bring him on in the correct way.

The exhibition bouts served a dual purpose. They protected Lewis, whose reputation was on the line with every promotion he staged, and they protected Wilde from the prospect of taking a beating from a bigger, more experienced opponent. Lewis did not have to wait long, however, to realise that his initial fears about Wilde were unfounded.

Jimmy's next reported outing at the Millfield Club was against Dai Thomas from Ystrad, a mining village just two miles from Tylorstown. Unlike Jimmy's other bouts, this would be a real fight.

Wilde overwhelmed Thomas from the sound of the opening bell. In the third round, with Thomas trapped on the ropes and being hit to both head and body, his corner wisely threw in the towel to save him from taking any further blows.

Teddy had arranged for a few of his boxers to fight on a promotion in Edinburgh and Jimmy's impressive performance against Thomas had convinced him that he was well and truly ready to fight further afield. When he asked Jimmy if he would like to fight in Edinburgh, he jumped at the chance. A trip to Scotland, a purse from the fight and money for travelling expenses. What was not to like!

Wilde boarded the train and set off northwards with Teddy and fellow boxers Young Dando from Cardiff, Dave Baxter from Pontypridd and Les Williams from Tonypandy.

On the night of the fights, the Olympic Palace in Edinburgh was full to its 2,000 capacity. Dando stopped his opponent in the

17th round. Baxter's fight with Syd Walker ended in the third round when Baxter, complaining of an injured left hand, gave the referee no option but to call the fight off and declare it a no-contest. Les Williams outpointed the delightfully named Tickler Lunt after 15 rounds, while Jimmy easily outsmarted Jim Easton of Glasgow over ten two-minute rounds.

The more familiar surroundings of the Millfield Hotel provided the venue for Jimmy's next contest. His opponent was Billy Bowen, who was a Tylorstown resident himself and outweighed Jimmy by some margin. Bowen was no match for Wilde, who did all the attacking from the start of the fight, and Bowen was forced to retire in the fourth.

It was not only Jimmy's exploits in the ring which were drawing attention. Elizabeth had sat at ringside for all of Jimmy's fights other than the one in Edinburgh. This had created quite a stir to say the least. It was unheard of for a woman to attend boxing shows at that time and Teddy tried on many occasions, through Jimmy, to persuade her not to attend. Elizabeth would hear none of it. She was going to support her husband, no matter what. In the end, Teddy had to accept the fact that Elizabeth Wilde was one person he could not get around.

Another impressive performance came against Young Jennings, who was from Dowlais, near Merthyr. Lewis took the fight on the understanding that Jennings would weigh 7st or under. It soon became obvious that Jennings was over the weight and would have no chance in shedding it in time. Jimmy did not mind. He told Lewis to take the fight anyway. Wilde put on a fine display of boxing. By the eighth round, Jennings's left eye was completely closed and his right eye was starting to swell shut as well. He gamely took all that Wilde could throw at him until the 11th, when the referee decided to stop the fight.

Teddy Lewis was more than pleased with Wilde's progress. He was now garnering quite a reputation in boxing circles in south Wales. Teddy knew that the lad had real talent and decided it was time to take him further afield. To Jimmy's delight, Teddy had booked him a fight in London at one of the capital's most famous boxing venues, the Ring.

The Ring was situated on Blackfriars Road in Southwark in south London and had originally been a chapel. A grand circular building with a polygon-shaped exterior, it was purchased by Dick Burge (the British lightweight champion from 1891–1897) and his wife, Bella. The building had been empty for some time and was dilapidated, but Dick and his wife were determined to make it a boxing arena suitable for the working man, unlike many of the capital's boxing venues, which were private members' clubs.

Dick and Bella persuaded local homeless people to clear it out and redecorate it. The Ring officially opened its doors on 14 May 1910 and boxing was held there on four nights a week. It quickly became a hotbed for south London boxing. Admittance was cheap and the building's unusual design gave the arena a unique, intimate atmosphere; the ring could be seen unhindered from any vantage point. To convey their thanks to the homeless people who had given the building a new lease of life, Dick and Bella kept the arena open during the daytime for use as a soup kitchen.

Wilde made his London debut on 20 January 1912. His opponent (who was the nephew of the reigning British lightweight champion, Matt Wells) fought under the *nom de guerre* Matt Wells' Nipper.

Teddy Lewis had taken the fight on the understanding that the Nipper would weigh no more than 7st on the night of the fight. Wilde weighed in at 6st 10lb, but, when the Nipper failed to show for the weigh-in, Lewis strongly suspected that the lad from Bow had struggled to make the weight.

It made no difference once the bell rang. Wilde planted a left into the Nipper's mid-section, causing him to lower his arms to protect his body. Wilde shot over a right to the chin and put the Nipper down. He rose to his feet on unsteady legs. Another right put the Nipper down for a second time. Gamely, the east Londoner managed to rise, but his equilibrium had gone. The referee, Mr J.T. Hulls, waved the fight off.

Wilde had impressed everyone. *Boxing* described him as 'the sensation of the evening'.[13] Many who were there thought it was the fight of the night, despite it only lasting around 90 seconds. Eleven days later, Wilde was fighting Young Baker at the Pudsey Street stadium in Liverpool. The crowd thought they were in for an early night when Wilde stunned the local man with the first punch of the fight, but Baker regained his composure and managed to survive until the final bell.

Despite Jimmy's success, Teddy was still concerned about his weight. Elizabeth made sure he ate extra portions of meat and

13 *Boxing* 27 January 1912

consumed plenty of eggs, but Jimmy still could not put on a single pound. As fate would have it, Jimmy's fast metabolism saved his life.

In the spring of 1912, Teddy had been speaking to the American fight agent Charlie Harvey, who had been looking to take a couple of Welsh boys over to fight in the States during the summer. As well as representing 'Peerless' Jim Driscoll (who was the British featherweight champion and Jimmy's close pal), Harvey also worked closely with the renowned promoter Tex Rickard, who would famously go on to steer Jack Dempsey to the world heavyweight title.

When Teddy told Jimmy about Harvey's plans, he enthusiastically put his name forward. Harvey told Wilde he would struggle to get a fight because there were no fighters at Jimmy's poundage in America. They were all bantamweights. Two other Welsh lads went instead.

Les Williams, a 23-year-old featherweight from Tonypandy, who was married with a young son, and his best friend, Dai Bowen, a 20-year-old featherweight from Treherbert, boarded RMS *Titanic* at Southampton as third class passengers on 10 April 1912, looking forward to the trip of a lifetime. They both perished when the liner sank five days later. Williams's body was later recovered and buried at sea a week after the tragedy. The body of Dai Bowen was never found. Many years later, Jimmy would recount how 'had I been given those extra pounds, I would have shared their fate' and how 'I shudder when I realise how desperately I tried to make Harvey change his mind'.[14]

14 Jimmy Wilde *Fighting Was My Business* p.69

Wilde's next bout was held in the open air on a balmy night in July at Cardiff stadium. Much to promoter Harry Duggan's delight, more than 2,000 people turned out to watch the show. Jimmy forced Kid Morris to retire at the end of the fifth round after he had been totally outclassed.

Jimmy then fought twice within five days at the Tonypandy Pavilion. Mike Flynn, a tough young fighter from Clydach Vale in the Rhondda, took him the full eight rounds and Jim Stuckey, who was 2st 4lb heavier than Wilde, also managed to go into the eighth, but he was stopped before the final bell.

Then came a series of quick wins. In Sheffield, Wilde outgunned Walter Heeley in three; Phil Davies was stopped in two at the Olympia Ice Rink in Merthyr; Young Rainsford, who had been courting a fight with Wilde for some time by issuing challenges in *Mirror of Life,* was stopped in the second after being put down in both rounds at Tonypandy; Mancunian Kid Pearson lasted only a round-and-a-half in Mountain Ash.

Young Hearn from south London was meant to be Wilde's next opponent at the Drill Hall in Pentre. Hearn had sent the promoters a wire that he was leaving London at 3pm that day, but by 9pm there was still no sign of him. The promoters, Evans and Kirkhouse, frantically scurried around looking for a suitable replacement. Thankfully, Alf Williams from Treherbert stepped in.

Williams outweighed Wilde by a massive 35lb and he had a fair punch on him. Wilde tore into him like a windmill from the first bell. Jimmy never gave the late substitute a moment's rest and, by the 11th round, it looked as if Williams was going down through exhaustion. To his immense credit, Williams dug deep and stood toe-to-toe with Jimmy in the 12th and final round. For the entire round, the crowd clapped in appreciation for his efforts at such short notice.

Stoker Staines proved to be no match for Wilde at Tonypandy and was dispatched in the first, even though Jimmy was suffering with a head cold. The Bargoed veteran Billy Yates was forced to retire in the fourth at the Theatre Royal in Cardiff a few days before Christmas on a night when the local fight fans were full of festive cheer. They gave Wilde a tremendous ovation when he entered the ring and were just as charitable when he left it.

When he first started boxing, Jimmy had two ambitions. One was to earn enough money from fighting so that he would be able to leave the mines for good. The other was to be able to buy a house for himself, Elizabeth and young David.

With his earnings from fighting boosting his wage from the colliery, Jimmy purchased a small terraced house at 20 Penrhys Avenue, a short walk from where they had lived with Dai and Sarah. The house cost £500. Jimmy took out a mortgage with the local building society, paying back £2 and ten shillings a month.

As soon as they had moved into their new home, Elizabeth made it her mission to reunite the Wilde family. For some time, Jimmy's younger brother and sister had been in the care of the Board of Guardians due to the difficulties between James and Margaret. Jimmy and Elizabeth visited the guardians to ask if Jimmy's brother and sister could now live with them. After a thorough interview – an ordeal that Jimmy and Elizabeth found more nerve-racking than any big fight – the board could clearly see that the two children would be living in a settled and caring environment. Permission to let them live with Jimmy and Elizabeth was granted.

The new year was looking bright. Teddy had a big fight lined up for Jimmy in January and, with the money that he had saved from his fights, leaving the mines and concentrating fully on boxing was now a distinct possibility.

5
Full-Time Fighter

ON 1 January 1913, Wilde travelled with Lewis and Jim Driscoll to Scotland for a fight against Glasgow's Young Billy Padden, a bout advertised as being for the '7st championship of Great Britain.'

The Victoria Athletic Club was packed to the rafters on the night. Earlier in the day, Padden had weighed in at 6st 13lb while Jimmy had come in 2lb lighter.

The fight, which was scheduled for 20 rounds, attracted a lot of side betting at ringside. Padden was a clever defensive boxer and many of the locals were banking on the Glaswegian being victorious.

From the opening bell, Wilde took the fight to Padden. Young Billy was prepared for this and was 'clever as always, slipping and ducking with coolness and excellent judgement'.[15]

In the second round, Padden weathered a heavy attack from Wilde and then got behind his jab. Wilde hurt Padden in the fifth with a heavy right to the side of the head, but Padden held on and then extricated himself from danger.

15 *Mirror of Life* 6 January 1913

After nine rounds of controlled boxing, the bout was even. Jimmy's blows carried more weight but, although Padden's punches were light, they were scoring points.

The weight of Wilde's blows had begun to tell on Padden by the 15th round. Sensing this, Wilde started to force Padden against the ropes and hit him with lefts and rights to the head.

As the bell sounded for the 17th round, Padden decided to change tack and go on the offensive. He had been boxing on the back foot, but now he met Jimmy head-on. This proved to be Billy's undoing. He threw a fast combination which Wilde managed to avoid. Wilde feinted and then threw a devastating uppercut which sent Padden to the canvas. Billy got up at the count of eight but another swift uppercut put him down for a second time. Bravely, Padden rose to his feet. He was now intent on survival. Wilde floored him again and Padden was saved by the bell.

The one-minute rest between rounds was never going to be enough for Padden. At the start of the 18th round, Wilde rushed out of his corner and threw another uppercut. Padden slumped to the canvas. This time he had nothing left. A sponge came flying into the ring from his cornerman, Young Snowball, to end the fight.

Padden's promoter apologised to Jimmy and Teddy for the crowd's partisan behaviour, which at times had threatened to get out of control. While Jimmy was unfazed, Teddy had become quite nervous during the bout. He had been sitting at the ringside in close proximity to the Scottish contingent and feared for his safety at one point.

Billy Padden was a full-time fighter, whereas Jimmy had been working at the colliery just 72 hours before the opening bell. When he arrived back home, he gave his £25 purse (worth around £2,400 in 2024 values) to Elizabeth. They talked it over and decided that now would be the right time for Jimmy to leave the mines and concentrate fully on boxing.

Wilde's decision pleased Teddy no end. He knew how talented Jimmy was and how much better he could become now that he could train without the burden of 12-hours shifts down the pit.

Living in such a tight-knit community as Tylorstown created its own worries for Jimmy. Ever since he had decided to leave the colliery and become a full-time boxer, he had been concerned about how his former workmates and other fighters who still worked in the pits would treat him. Jimmy knew more than anyone the struggles that a pit man faced and the last thing he wanted was to be perceived as leaving them behind. Thankfully, every miner and fellow fighter he came into contact with in Tylorstown and the surrounding villages endorsed his decision and gave him their full support.

Teddy quickly arranged for Jimmy's training headquarters to be on the top floor of the Tylorstown Working Men's Club in East Street. An added bonus was that downstairs there was a full-size snooker table on which Jimmy and his pals whiled away many hours when not training.

After his fight against Padden in Glasgow, 12 of Wilde's next 13 fights were closer to home in Tonypandy.

On 18 January, Wilde fought Blackburn's Tommy Hughes, who was billed as the '7st champion of the North West'. Hughes was a tremendously tough lad who took everything that Wilde threw at him in the opening round. He was groggy going back to his corner after the opening three minutes and was knocked down in the fourth and fifth. The Lancastrian earned loud applause for his courage in the sixth before the referee, Ralph Lisle, stopped the fight in the seventh.

In his next bout, Wilde gave away more than a stone in weight to Dick Jenkins. This fight was under the 'no decision' rule. The only way either fighter could win was by registering a knockout. Jimmy tried, but he could not get through the watertight defence of the ultra-negative Jenkins, who clinched his way to the final bell.

Young Fitzpatrick was stopped in three rounds and then Jimmy fought Porth's Dai Mathews. The promoter took it upon himself to advertise Mathews as the '8st champion of Wales' even though he had always been around the 7st mark and was nowhere near championship class. This was proven when the fight started. The first punch Wilde landed bloodied Mathews's nose. He was knocked down in the fourth and his corner decided that he had taken enough and threw in the towel.

On Easter Monday 1913, Wilde took on Harry Taylor and the Swansea man was no match for his lighter adversary. Wilde felled him in the second and third. Taylor retired on his stool before the start of the fourth.

Will Rees from Mountain Ash had a 2st weight advantage over Wilde when they met on 12 April. Rees was a hard puncher and he stunned Jimmy a few times in the first round. Rees, who had sustained a cut over his eye while fighting the previous week, was proving to be a tricky customer, but a left from Wilde reopened the cut and Rees completely lost his composure from that moment. Jimmy swarmed all over him and stopped him in the second.

A week later, Wilde had a rematch with Billy Yates. Wilde had originally been set to meet Stoker Hoskyne, but he had to pull out and a replacement had to be found at short notice. Their second match went the same way as the first. Yates was counted out in the fourth.

On the same bill that night, Jimmy's cousin, Dai 'Chips' Davies, fought a draw with Manny Chamberlain. Davies would be Jimmy's next opponent.

There had been talk of a fight between the two for some time. Folk in Tylorstown were split as to who to support. It was a big fight in Tylorstown and both men were given five weeks to prepare for it.

In front of a seething, expectant crowd at the Tonypandy Pavilion, Davies gave Wilde an even tougher fight than Padden had done.

Jimmy got off to a fast start. By the third round. Davies's eye was swollen shut. In his corner between rounds, Jim Driscoll told Wilde to target it.

In the sixth, a barrage of punches from Davies made Jimmy retreat to the ropes. Davies rained blows on Jimmy. The sheer volume of them sent Wilde through the ropes and out of the ring!

Shakily, Wilde made it back in time and was able to survive. The swollen eye that Davies had sustained was proving to be a real handicap for him. For the next four rounds, both fought as if their lives depended on it. Wilde scored repeatedly with blows that Davies could not see coming. After 20 minutes of gruelling action, the bell rang to signal the end of the fight. Many at ringside thought that, had it not been for his closed eye, 'Chips' would have won.

The fact that both boys were from the same town had undoubtedly contributed to the fierce nature of the fight. The two little warriors had put on a fine spectacle and they were the best of mates again as the verdict was announced.

After such a gruelling encounter, Wilde did not fight again for three weeks. Nevertheless, his next opponent would not be any easier. A return match with Billy Padden was arranged for 14 June at the pavilion in Tonypandy.

On the night of the fight, there was a full house. Well over 100 unlucky spectators were locked out and had to rely on receiving updates of how the fight was going from those inside.

After his stellar showing in their first bout, Padden was again expected to give Wilde a hard time.

Padden made a slower start than he had done in Glasgow and was floored by a left to the body in the opening round. Padden regained his composure in the next two rounds and drew appreciative applause for his fast double jabs.

Wilde totally dominated the fourth round, forcing Padden to take three counts, but the Glasgow man recovered well enough to take the fifth with his crisp lefts. Padden was down again in the sixth, but rallied in the following three rounds. He matched Wilde punch for punch in a desperate effort to stay with him.

In the tenth, Padden was floored twice – once after taking a left hook to the chin, the second time after a left to the chest took the wind out of him.

Wilde knocked Padden over again in the 11th. He was definitely wilting, but he refused to buckle. Realising that he was behind, Padden came on strong in the remainder of the round and continued in the same vein in the 12th. Wilde narrowly missed him with an uppercut that would have ended the fight had it landed, but Padden gave everything he had until the final bell.

Once again, Padden had shown tremendous heart and courage. The Tonypandy crowd, unlike their Glasgow counterparts, gave the visitor a standing ovation at the end of the fight.

The boxing shows in Tonypandy were proving to be extremely popular. The promoters were pitting local lads against each other in even, value-for-money match-ups. The popularity of the shows was such that the seating area had to be expanded to accommodate the ever-increasing crowds.

When Jimmy fought Tommy Lewis in July at the pavilion, there were three fighters on the bill from Tylorstown alone – Jimmy, Dai 'Chips' Davies and Young Purnell. Tylorstown was by no means unique in this regard. Each town in the Rhondda had at least four or five boxers who plied their trade week in, week out across south Wales.

On 4 August, Darkie Saunders came to the Cardiff skating rink to fight Wilde in a ten-round contest. Jimmy easily outpointed the Camberwell-based West Indian.

Next up for Jimmy was a fight at the Pudsey Street stadium. His opponent, Jack Dyer, outweighed Wilde by 22lb, but the slugger from St Helens was too crude and could not put his extra weight to good use. Wilde knocked him down in the third and the referee, seeing that Dyer was unable to continue, dispensed with the count halfway through.

Dido Gains was billed as one of London's best flyweights. He met Wilde on 8 September in Cardiff and was expected to give him a stern test. Gains had two outstanding wins to his name, having beaten the top-rated Alf Mansfield and Joe Symonds.

Wilde was giving away 16lb in weight to Gains and he uncharacteristically started the fight by throwing roundhouse swings. Gains was fairly wild with his punches, but both men soon settled into the contest and it was Wilde's clever footwork and fast left-right combinations that enabled him to win a comfortable decision after 15 two-minute rounds.

A return fight with George Dando took place on 22 September. Wilde had easily outpointed the man from Merthyr when they met three months earlier, but Dando made more of a fight of it the second time around. *Boxing* reported that 'Wilde had to exert all his ring craft and to pull out all his skills to break level during the early rounds'.[16]

---

16 *Boxing* 27 September 1913

Dando shook Wilde in the 16th with a right to the jaw that had Teddy Lewis worried, but Jimmy got his boxing back together and did enough to get the decision. After the fight, Wilde told the assembled reporters how he had badly hurt his hand early in the fight and that he had relied solely on his left jab to get him over the line.

Wilde was out of action for six weeks after the Dando fight with a damaged metacarpal. He kept in shape by running and shadow boxing. Sometimes he would tell Elizabeth to don a big pair of boxing gloves and throw punches at him while he dodged and ducked around the living room. By early November, his hand had healed sufficiently for him to return to the ring.

A second meeting with Darkie Saunders was promptly arranged and Wilde was back to his best, stopping Saunders in the 11th round. *Boxing* described Wilde's performance as being 'one of the most dashing he has ever given'.[17]

Wilde then went over old ground by beating Young Baker in ten rounds and Jack Dyer in two. Poor Dyer put up such little resistance that Wilde fought again the following night in Swansea. In front of 2,000 spectators, Wilde outpointed Dido Gains over 15 rounds.

The Welsh promoters were keen to see a third fight between Wilde and George Dando. They set it for 6 December at the Drill Hall in Merthyr, which was Dando's backyard. Wilde boxed his way into an unassailable lead by winning the first nine rounds. In the tenth, Wilde and Dando came together in a clinch. Dando

17 *Boxing* 8 November 1913

was bearing all his weight down on Wilde, which forced him to one knee. Instead of taking a step back and waiting for Jimmy to rise, Dando hit him on the side of the head. Without hesitating, referee Lisle took Dando to a neutral corner and signalled to the ringside officials that he had disqualified him. It was a testament to the sportsmanship of the crowd that they graciously accepted the decision without causing any trouble, especially as it was their man who had transgressed.

In his next fight, Jimmy conceded 24lb in weight to Billy Charles. Wilde darted in and out, scoring with fast left jabs before Charles had an opportunity to hold and use his extra weight to his advantage. The man from Bargoed had to retire in the sixth after 'he had taken a lot of punishment from a world beater'.[18]

Ten days before Christmas, Wilde capped off a busy year by fighting Harry Brookes in Manchester. The handbill for the evening's boxing labelled Wilde 'The Mighty Atom'. This was the first time that this sobriquet was used for Wilde and it stuck. Brooks was knocked down in the second, the fourth, twice in the eighth and once in the ninth. Wisely, he remained seated on his stool as the bell rang for round ten. *Boxing* described the fight as being 'a procession from start to finish'.[19]

18 *Boxing* 20 December 1913
19 *Boxing* 27 December 1913

6

Debut At HQ

WILDE STARTED 1914 with a 15-round points win over Albert 'Ginger' Nutter on 3 January at the Marquee in Tonypandy. The light-punching lad from Preston was defensively clever and ducked and slipped his way to the final bell.[20]

Teddy Lewis now had his sights firmly set on Wilde challenging for the British flyweight title, but Jimmy's great friend Percy Jones, who was from nearby Porth, had first crack at Bill Ladbury's crown. Jones, who was seven months younger than Wilde, was himself from a mining family and had learnt his trade on the boxing booths in and around Tonypandy. Wilde was prepared to wait for his chance. He and Percy had agreed they would never fight each other.[21]

Five days after beating Nutter, Wilde went to Liverpool, where he fought Young Beynon from Merthyr. Beynon, who

20 Nutter later joined the 7th Battalion Royal North Lancashire Regiment and was killed in action at High Wood, the Somme, on 22 July 1916.

21 Jones joined the Welsh Fusiliers in 1915. The following year he was badly injured in the leg at the Somme and was medically discharged. In 1918 his leg had to be amputated. Jones died of blood poisoning on Christmas Day 1922. He would have been 30 the following day. Ladbury joined the Royal West Kent Regiment and was killed in action on 18 June 1917 at Flanders. He was 28.

had recently gone the distance with Jones, started off well behind his jab but, from the second round onwards, it was all Wilde. He floored Beynon twice in the ninth and once in the tenth, 11th and 13th. Beynon, who was as tough as they come, somehow got through the next two rounds. Wilde had won every round.

On 29 January, Wilde returned to Liverpool to fight Billy Padden for a third time. Jimmy knocked Padden out of his stride with his left jab in the first round and put the Scot over in the second. Padden was saved by the bell. In the third round, Padden was still feeling the effects of Wilde's punches. A quick combination forced him to the ropes and the referee was left no option but to stop the fight. Afterwards, Padden told *Boxing* he was 'amazingly surprised at the improvement in the boy since our last fight'.[22]

In February 1914, Wilde astonishingly had four fights in just 16 days. Albert 'Ginger' Nutter was comfortably outpointed again in Birkenhead on 2 February. Seven days later, Wilde was at the Free Trade Hall in Manchester, flooring Tom Thomas seven times before the referee, Tom Gamble, waved off the fight in the seventh.

On 12 February, Wilde took on Liverpudlian Paddy Carroll at Pudsey Street. Carroll was a wily veteran who was known for his durability. He had fought Sid Smith three times and had taken the ex-champion the distance on each occasion. Sadly, Carroll was on the wane by the time he fought Wilde. His last three losses had all come inside the distance. Wilde knocked down the brave Scouser midway through the second round. Carroll gallantly

22 *Boxing* 7 February 1914

rose at six, but his punch resistance had gone. Another barrage of blows from Wilde put him down again. Carroll never looked as if he was going to get up and was counted out.

Four days later, Wilde crossed the Pennines to Sheffield to fight Chesterfield's George Jaggers at the Drill Hall. Jaggers outweighed Wilde by 20lb, but it had no bearing on the result of the bout. Jaggers found himself on the canvas twice in the second round and retired with an injured hand in the fifth.

Bill Kyne, from Poplar in east London, was a tough fighter who had gone the distance with fighters of the calibre of Bill Ladbury, Percy Jones and Joe Symonds. Fighting Wilde, though, was a different proposition. Kyne, normally so durable, was totally outfought and outclassed in a fourth-round stoppage.

Wilde's fight against Kyne had been a perfect warm-up for him. Just four days later, he would be making his debut at the headquarters of British boxing, the National Sporting Club, against his first overseas opponent.

The National Sporting Club opened on 5 March 1891. Located at 43 King Street in Covent Garden, the NSC came into being due to the closure of the Pelican Club, which had opened four years earlier in Gerard Street, Soho.

The Pelican Club had staged illegal prize fights and had survived mainly because its patrons were of high rank. The Pelican could not shake off its rowdy, bohemian reputation, though. Soon after it staged a world title fight between America's George Dixon and England's Nunc Wallace in 1891, the Pelican started to wind down and eventually closed later that year.

The two men who had managed the Pelican Club, A.F. 'Peggy' Bettinson (a former ABA lightweight champion in 1882) and John Fleming (a publican and matchmaker) soon found new premises and the National Sporting Club came into being.

Bettinson and Fleming were determined to make the NSC a respectable boxing establishment with a strict code of conduct for both its members and the boxers. To give the club even more clout, Bettinson asked Hugh Lowther, the fifth Earl of Lonsdale, to be the club's president. It was a role Lowther accepted without hesitation.

Every Monday evening, professional men dressed in dinner jackets would head to the NSC in King Street. Entering the club through its ornate lobby, they would climb the mahogany staircase to the bar and restaurant. After a sumptuous meal, usually fillet steak or Dover sole, the members would make their way downstairs to the fight hall. There, the members would take their seat, light a cigar and talk among themselves until the first preliminary bout of the evening was due to commence. Either Fleming or Bettinson would climb into the ring to introduce the two boxers and then politely remind members that there must be silence during the fights and that they could only speak during the interval between rounds.

The National Sporting Club, as Bettinson had intended, dictated who the national champions were and who was eligible to challenge for titles. If a boxer's manager had a good relationship with Bettinson, his fighter would be allowed to fight there. On the other hand, if a fighter had a manager who had rocked the boat, he would have to settle for a career in the provinces with little or no recognition, irrespective of his talent.

The committee at the NSC was anxious to distance itself from the London Prize Ring of old and revised the Queensberry Rules. Gloves were to be worn at all times and would weigh no less than 4oz each, the ring was to be between 14 and 20ft square and all fights were to last no longer than 15 rounds (except championship bouts, which were 20). To eliminate any skulduggery, a boxer's seconds were only allowed in the ring during the one-minute rest period between rounds.

In February 1909, the National Sporting Club became the first boxing regulatory body to standardise the weights in the seven divisions that had survived from the bare-knuckle era. They also introduced a new division – flyweight.

Boxing in Britain now had a strict weight structure: flyweight (8st); bantamweight (8st 6lb); featherweight (9st); lightweight (9st 9lb); welterweight (10st 7lb); middleweight (11st 6lb); light heavyweight (12st 7lb) and heavyweight (over 12st 7lb).

That same year, Lord Lonsdale introduced the Lord Lonsdale challenge belt. This would be awarded to the British champion in each weight division. Now everyone would know who the champions were. It finally put an end to the time-honoured tradition of several fighters *claiming* to be the best at their weight. A fighter could only fight for – and retain – the belt by fighting at the National Sporting Club. If a fighter won three bouts with the belt at stake, it would be his to keep.

On 30 March 1914, Wilde made his first appearance at the National Sporting Club against the virtually unknown, light-hitting Frenchman Eugene Husson.

Despite his reputation for beating bigger men, Bettinson had misgivings about putting Wilde on the bill due to his small stature. In an act of extreme caution, Bettinson found, through French manager Francois Deschamps, an opponent for Wilde who was even smaller. For one of the few times in his career, Wilde was bigger than the fighter he was facing. At 4ft 10in, Husson was four inches shorter than Wilde and weighed 6st 3lb, half a stone lighter.

Mirror of Life described Husson as 'about the smallest andmost delicate little warrior that had ever climbed between the ropes'.[23]

In the first round, Wilde had great difficulty trying to catch the Parisian as he skirted around the perimeter of the ring. Husson had definitely been forewarned about Wilde's punching power.

The second round followed the same pattern, but Wilde was beginning to get through with the odd punch to Husson's body.

In the third, Husson threw a right and, to the astonishment of those in the hall, Wilde countered with a left of his own over Husson's extended right arm and shook the Frenchman to his heels.

By the fourth, Husson was starting to feel the effects of Wilde's body punches. Wilde caught Husson with a left, forcing him to one knee for a seven count. Husson survived, but he was put down again in the fifth when Wilde caught him with a right to the jaw. Husson bravely got to his feet and retreated

23 *Mirror of Life* 4 April 1914

to the ropes, where he ducked, bobbed and weaved his way out of danger.

The crowd sensed it was now only a matter of time before Husson would crumble. In the sixth round, Wilde bided his time until he saw an opening and put Husson over with a right cross. Husson resembled a puppet that had had its strings cut as he crumpled to the canvas. The referee stood over him counting to ten, even though it was obvious that he was never going to beat the count.

7
Contender

WILDE'S PERFORMANCE against Eugene Husson had taken the National Sporting Club by storm. 'Peggy' Bettinson, who had initially been reluctant to have Wilde appear, was now champing at the bit to get him back as soon as possible.

Two weeks after his stellar showing in the capital, Wilde was in Ashton-under-Lyne to take on Jack Madden at the Portland Street ice rink.

The promoters of the show, Cropper and Dalton, described Madden on the handbill as 'one of the most scientific boxers Lancashire has ever produced'. In reality, Madden was a limited fighter who was never going to go the 15-round distance the bout was scheduled for.

As soon as the fight started, it was obvious there was a gulf in class between the two men. Wilde, with his hands by his waist, feinted and shuffled around in the first, sizing up Madden. In the second round, Wilde realised Madden's punches were too slow and he started to score with heavy left and right-hand counters. Madden took more punishment in the third before being dropped and counted out in the fourth.

Teddy Lewis was intent on keeping Wilde busy, but he also wanted him to be tested. Frenchman Albert Bouzzonie, Teddy hoped, would fit the bill.

Bouzzonie had made his debut in 1910 and had fought mainly at the Wonderland arena in Paris. In 1912, he made his first foray abroad when he travelled to London and lost a ten-round decision to British flyweight champion Sid Smith. Two moths later, Smith outpointed Bouzzonie again, this time in Paris. Bouzzonie, a squat, muscular man who was built more like a bodybuilder, with short bulging biceps and forearms, had then lost a close decision to his talented countryman Eugene Criqui.[24]

On 16 April 1914, the Pudsey Street stadium was brimming with fight fans who were all eager to see Wilde take on his second foreign opponent in as many weeks.

Bouzzonie (8st) came out firing. He rocked Wilde (6st 10lb) with a few hard combinations to the head that had him in trouble. A big right from Bouzonnie knocked down Wilde. He sprang up quickly on rubbery legs and hung on until the end of the round.

The Frenchman, who was by far the stronger man, continued to land heavy blows in the second. In the third, Wilde decided to meet fire with fire. He stood toe-to-toe with Bouzzonie, who refused to take a backward step. The crowd roared their approval as both men went back to their corners at the end of the round.

---

24 Criqui joined the French Army in 1915 and had his jaw shattered by a bullet. His jaw was rebuilt and amazingly he returned to the ring in 1917. Criqui won the world featherweight title in 1923 from Johnny Kilbane but lost it 54 days later to Johnny Dundee. Criqui died in France in 1977. He was 84.

In the fourth, both continued to work in close. Bouzzonie was doing most of the punching, with Wilde content to slip and block as many of the punches as he could.

In the fifth, Bouzzonie came out throwing wild, roundhouse punches that repeatedly fell short. Wilde would then score with sharp lefts and, by the time Bouzzonie was ready to throw shots back, would be out of range. Bouzzonie was intent on knocking Wilde out. *Boxing* described Wilde's boxing as 'coolness personified'.[25]

The Frenchman had put everything he had into the first five rounds. In the sixth, he gave one last, big effort. He chased after Wilde, hoping to land one knockout blow, but Wilde was now counter-punching to great effect. Wilde made Bouzzonie miss and landed a right that shook him to his boots. Bouzzonie retreated to the ropes where Wilde rained blow after blow on him. Bouzonnie swayed left and right, taking everything that Wilde could throw at him until the bell rang to end the round. As he tottered back to his corner, Bouzzonie looked over his shoulder to the referee and waved his hand in a sign of surrender.

It had been a wildly exciting fight which proved Wilde could take a tremendous punch, get knocked down and, most importantly, get back up and go on to win.

There is no doubt Wilde had taken some serious wallops from Bouzzonie. He could have done with a couple of weeks off, but the idea of rest was anathema to Teddy Lewis. Just over a week after his fight with Bouzzonie, Wilde was back in the

25 *Boxing* 25 April 1914

ring with arguably the most experienced man he had faced in his career so far.

Alf Mansfield was a bantamweight from Aldgate in the East End of London. He turned pro in 1910, fighting mostly at the Judean Athletic Club, where he became good friends with Ted 'Kid' Lewis. Mansfield and Lewis, who shared the same boarding house for a time, would sell newspapers together in Whitechapel to boost their ring earnings.

By the time he fought Wilde, Mansfield had taken part in more than 90 fights and had mixed in top-class company. In 1912, he had fought a draw with Eugene Criqui in Paris and, the following year, had taken Joe Symonds the distance.

Mansfield's most frequent opponent was Dido Gains. With Mansfield living in Aldgate and Gains residing just over the river in Lambeth, it was a natural rivalry that always drew a crowd. They fought each other seven times; Mansfield won three and Gains one, with three drawn.

Mansfield was a true pro and as game as they come. He had travelled all over the country fighting men in their own backyards. He never took a backward step and was one of those fighters who would take three punches in order to land one of his own.

Three thousand people turned out to see the fight at the Olympia ice rink in Leeds. What they did not know was that Teddy Lewis had only agreed to take the fight on the proviso that Mansfield, who had fought Billy Nutts at 8st 6lb the previous week, boil himself down to 7st 10lb. This left the Aldgate man with the unenviable task of losing 11lb in four days.

Mansfield took to the Turkish baths and jogged around wearing three pullovers. Each bead of sweat that fell from his head was torture. Each droplet that fell to the ground was making him weaker.

Lewis had been adamant that Mansfield must lose the weight. At the weigh-in on the afternoon of the fight, a drawn, pensive Mansfield weighed in at 7st 11lb. That one extra pound would not come off. Rather than call off the bout, a compromise was reached. The fight was on.

There is no doubt Mansfield was severely handicapped by having to shed so much weight in such a short space of time. The fight, which had promised to be a highly competitive one, turned out to be a damp squib.

Wilde dominated with his left jab. Mansfield, who unsurprisingly had no energy whatsoever, did nothing of note until the fourth round when he managed to put a short burst of light punches together.

By the tenth, Mansfield was bleeding from a nasty cut on his lip. Somehow, Mansfield dragged his bone-dry body through the next ten rounds, using all of his experience to cover up and evade Wilde's non-stop combinations. It had been the longest 40 minutes of his life.

For his next promotion at the National Sporting Club on 11 May 1914, 'Peggy' Bettinson pitted three British boxers against three from France. The former world bantamweight champion Joe Bowker fought Robert Dastillon, Young Greenstock fought Marcel Denis and Wilde's opponent was Georges Gloria.

Gloria, whose real name was Georges Vitard, had beaten the great Georges Carpentier when they were both at the start of their careers and campaigning as bantamweights. Carpentier would carry on growing and win the world light-heavyweight title and unsuccessfully challenge the great Jack Dempsey for the heavyweight crown. Gloria, however, stopped growing and would never fight above featherweight.

Gloria had fought exclusively in Paris and the surrounding provinces. After a promising start, his career had fallen into a pattern of winning a few and then losing a few.

The trip to London was a daunting prospect for him. Not only was he fighting Wilde, it would also be the first time he had fought outside of his home country.

The fight turned out to be totally one-sided. Wilde won the opening four rounds with his left jab alone, which not only reddened the Frenchman's face but prevented him from getting himself set to mount any worthwhile attacks of his own.

In the fifth, Wilde landed a right to Gloria's head. Jimmy immediately felt a sharp pain shoot up from his thumb into his wrist. When he got back to his corner at the end of the round, he told Driscoll about it. Driscoll urged him not to worry. He could win the fight with just his left.

Gloria's punches had no power or snap behind them. When he did manage to land with the odd combination, they did not even seem to register with Wilde, who was controlling the pace of the fight. It was a chastening experience for the man from Paris. He protested when the referee stopped the fight in the ninth round, but it was a false act of bravado. Inside, he would have been relieved that his ordeal was over.

Boxing was fulsome in its praise. 'There isn't a flyweight in the world today, and we are not sure if there are many, if any, bantams, who could hold a candle to the mighty terror from Tylorstown.'[26]

Wilde was pleased with his performance, but his main concern was his injured thumb. It had hurt during the fight, but the pain was significantly worse afterwards when the adrenaline subsided. Within a few hours, he was unable to make a fist. After a thorough examination, it was confirmed that Wilde had broken his thumb.

Needing time to heal, Wilde found himself on the sidelines. He kept in trim by running around after young David and by asking Elizabeth to don a large pair of boxing gloves and throw punches at him. It was not ideal, but it helped him retain a modicum of sharpness.

While Jimmy was out of action, the landscape of the flyweight division changed. Percy Jones, who had won the British title from Bill Ladbury, was forced to vacate the title because he could no longer make 8st. The division was now wide open. Wilde, Joe Symonds and Scotsman Tancy Lee – who had beaten Tommy Harrison in a final eliminator – were now the main challengers for the coveted Lonsdale belt.

After six weeks out of the ring, Wilde returned to action on 22 June at the Market Hall in Aberdare against Charlie Banyard, a capable fighter from Fulham in west London.

26 *Boxing* 16 May 1914

Teddy Lewis had seen Banyard fight a couple of times before and considered him to be the perfect comeback opponent for Wilde. He could give Wilde rounds without posing too much of a threat.

Banyard, who had a weight advantage of 21lb, was never allowed to get into the fight. Wilde was too fast for him. Banyard was floored twice in the sixth, once in the eighth and twice in the ninth before the referee, Charlie Barrett, stopped it. After the fight, Wilde was not so much pleased with the win as relieved that he had felt no pain in his right hand.

Lambeth bantamweight Charlie Lorden showed an almost superhuman ability to absorb punishment when he fought Wilde at Tonypandy in July. To the amazement of the large crowd, the Londoner lasted into the 11th round before he was forced to turn away in surrender from another onslaught of punches.

Five days later, Wilde fought an American for the first time. Artie Edwards, who had boxed mainly in the fight clubs of New York, was booked to meet Wilde and then fight Alf Mansfield. Despite Edwards's 'win some, lose some' record against fighters who were mostly from his home state, many scribes felt Wilde would have a fight on his hands.

Wilde 'gave the spectators a marvellous display of ringcraft'. His left jab 'beat a constant tattoo on Edwards's face' and the visitor was looking disconsolate in his corner at the end of the fifth round.[27]

27 *Boxing* 1 August 1914

The Liverpool crowd were strongly behind Wilde, but they were fair nonetheless. They realised Edwards was having a tough time and admired his grit and determination in lasting the distance.

Many boxing writers now considered Wilde unbeatable. Some wrote that they wished he had grown to be a heavyweight. Despite having great fighters in the lower weight divisions, Britain still craved a world heavyweight champion above all else.

Nearly a quarter of a century later, Wilde modestly expressed his thoughts on how the sporting press had taken to him. 'It was slowly percolating in my mind that I was becoming an attraction in the real meaning of the word. It was a grand realisation. It would be absurd to pretend that I did not enjoy it to the full.'[28]

Sport was proving to be a welcome distraction from the growing troubles on the continent. On 4 August 1914, King George V solemnly informed the nation that war had been declared on Germany after it ignored Britain's ultimatum not to invade neutral Belgium.

In south Wales, young men were being urged to go to their local military office to join up. Lord Kitchener's poster, with the slogan 'Your King and Country Needs You', implored young men to enlist. In Glamorgan, the Red Cross appealed for donations to help buy 1,000 beds for when the injured returned home. Barracks were hastily being built all over the country to house thousands of newly trained soldiers.

28 Jimmy Wilde *Fighting Was My Business* p.75

It was amidst this feeling of gloom and uncertainty that Wilde travelled to St James Hall in Newcastle to fight Jarrow's Young Walters. Walters accidentally hit Wilde low in the second. The punch did not unduly bother him but, when Walters strayed low again in the sixth round, the referee, to the crowd's dismay, instantly disqualified him.

By the time Wilde returned home, the National Sporting Club had announced that he would be fighting Joe Symonds in November in a final eliminator. The winner would face Tancy Lee for the vacant British flyweight title.

In the meantime, Teddy Lewis arranged for Wilde to have a return match with Alf Mansfield, who had recently outpointed Artie Edwards in Wallsend.

Crucially for Mansfield, this time he would not be required to drastically make weight.

Both men were trained to perfection. Mansfield, who was at full strength weighing 8st 2lb, started briskly. Wilde (6st 12lb) darted out of danger as Mansfield constantly came forward.

The early rounds were cagey and belonged to the Londoner, just. In the sixth and seventh, Wilde sensed that Mansfield was tiring and found his distance and timing. Wilde's right-hand punches were now starting to find their mark. Every time Mansfield threw a punch, Wilde would skip out of harm's way and then reply with three or four hurtful counters. Mansfield was now 'a punching bag from gong to gong'.[29]

---

29 *Sporting Life* 29 September 1914

In the tenth round, Mansfield's cornermen, knowing that their man was struggling, humanely threw in the towel. Wilde went over to Mansfield's corner and embraced him. Mansfield, bruised and battered, forced a smile and wished Jimmy the best of luck for his fight with Symonds.

8

The Plymouth Prodigy

JOE SYMONDS was born Hubert Toms on 28 December 1894 in Plymouth. He started boxing as a young boy and assumed the ring name of 'Young' Joe Symonds when he had his first professional fight in 1910.

During the next three years, Symonds fought exclusively at the Cosmopolitan gym in Plymouth against local boys from Devon.

The 'Cosmo', as it was called by the locals, had opened in 1907 when Billy Bennett, Harold Williams and Silas Algar purchased a run-down old storage building and converted it into a boxing gym. With the help of promoter Bob Dorman, who himself owned a boxing club in London called the Cosmopolitan, the 'Cosmo' soon became Plymouth's premier boxing venue.

Symonds's first opponent of note was Alf Mansfield, who Symonds outpointed on 3 March 1913. Later that same month, Symonds fought Percy Jones in Tonypandy. The fight was an even one until, in the fourth round, the referee disqualified Symonds for a low blow. This had a whiff of a hometown decision about it. Symonds's manager, Harry Jenkins, was so incensed that he immediately offered Jones £25 for a rematch.

Undeterred, Symonds won four fights in a row and then took on the British flyweight champion Sid Smith in a non-title bout. Smith piled up points with his left jab and was a comprehensive, if unspectacular, winner after 15 rounds.

Symonds had certainly not disgraced himself with his performance against Smith. Just over a fortnight later, Symonds got his rematch with Percy Jones in a ten-rounder at the National Sporting Club. This time, Jones left nothing to chance. An unusually lacklustre Symonds lost a clear decision.

On 2 March 1914, Symonds fought ex-British champion Bill Ladbury at New Cross Baths in London. Ladbury was down twice in the fifth and, although Ladbury staged a late rally in the last five rounds while being loudly cheered on by his local supporters, many thought Symonds had done enough to win. There were audible gasps of astonishment when the MC announced that the result was a draw.

On 15 May 1914, Symonds fought Percy Jones again at the 'Cosmo'. Jones, however, was now an ex-champion. He had been forced to hand back his Lonsdale belt because he was unable to get down to the championship weight. An inspired Symonds knocked out the crestfallen Welshman in the 18th round.

Symonds was now on the cusp of title contention. During the summer, he solidified his claim by outboxing the durable Tommy Harrison from Hanley and getting a disqualification win over Albert Bouzonnie, who was thrown out in the seventh for persistent holding. The National Sporting Club wasted little time in nominating Symonds and Wilde as a final eliminator, with the winner to meet Tancy Lee for the vacant crown.

During the build-up to the fight with Symonds, George Baillieu (who had helped train Jim Driscoll) was brought on board to help oversee training while Driscoll was otherwise engaged training Percy Jones.

Baillieu decided that it would be a good idea for Wilde to train away from home, a decision which Jimmy and Elizabeth were not happy about. Throughout his career, Elizabeth had always been close by. Now she was only allowed to visit her husband once a week.

The Esplanade Hotel on the Porthcawl seafront was Wilde's training base from the last week of October until the day of the fight. Wilde would start his day with a brisk walk along the pier, taking in lungfuls of bracing sea air, before going back to the hotel for breakfast.

In the early afternoon, Wilde and Baillieu, along with Jimmy's sparring partners, would make the short journey to the Victoria Hotel, where the manager had converted the top floor into a gym.

There, Wilde went through his programme of stretching, hitting the speedball and sparring three rounds each with Tylorstown bantamweight Billie Fry and Porth's Dickie Morgan. After the six rounds of sparring, Wilde did his calisthenics on the floor to strengthen his legs, arms and stomach. Then, after a quick warm-down, it was back to the Esplanade for dinner and a quiet evening playing cards with his sparring mates.

Although he would be giving away more than a stone in weight, the general consensus among the boxing press was that Wilde would be too skilful for Symonds.

Despite the feeling that Wilde would prevail, *The Sportsman* cautioned that Wilde would be 'tackling perhaps the hardest proposition he has ever undertaken'.[30]

Wilde was in a confident mood. 'I hear they [the Symonds camp] have some tactics up their sleeve to checkmate some of my well-known moves. Well, you can take it from me that, barring a lucky punch, I have a very good chance, see.'[31]

Teddy Lewis was on edge, though. With Percy Jones's recent weight problems, Lewis had been forced to pay a heavy forfeit to the NSC. Things had got worse for him in Porthcawl. One of Teddy's other fighters, Llew Edwards, was forced to cancel his fight with Young Brookes after he sprained his ankle on a training run, which meant another forfeit had to be paid. Teddy was praying that the odds for Wilde would be generous enough for him to recoup his losses and cover the expenses.

On the afternoon of the fight, Wilde and Symonds weighed in at the NSC. Symonds, standing in just his underpants, weighed 7st 13lb. Wilde, who was fully clothed and wearing a flat cap, got on the scales. 'Well inside,' shouted Bettinson. 'Let it go at that.'

A few hours later, both men were in their respective corners getting gloved-up. Symonds, wearing a grey dressing gown, looked

30 *The Sportsman* 14 November 1914
31 *Sporting Life* 16 November 1914

a picture of health when he disrobed. With the help of trainer Sam French, the Plymouth man, whose record was 43-7-5, came to the ring in peak condition. Wilde, wearing a navy blue dressing gown, looked confident and focused. Sitting at ringside were Jimmy's stablemates Percy Jones and Llew Edwards, alongside fellow contenders Sid Smith, Bill Ladbury and Tancy Lee.

The first round was cagey, with lots of feinting. Neither man was willing to commit himself too much at such an early stage. In the second round, Symonds drew hoots of derision from the crowd as he twice hit Wilde low. As the bell rang to end the round, Symonds hit Wilde below the belt again.

Inexplicably, he hit Wilde low again in the third with a punch that 'could be heard all over the club'.[32] Wilde, to his credit, kept his composure and stuck to his boxing. The crowd was losing patience with Symonds and hissed at him when the bell rang at the end of the round.

In the fourth, Symonds managed to keep his punches up. Wilde scored at will with his left jab in what was a quieter round than the preceding ones. Symonds's mouth started bleeding in the fifth. Wilde cleverly blocked and parried most of Symonds's punches and the man from Plymouth, his face smeared crimson, looked confused as he went back to his corner.

The sixth and seventh were Wilde's by a big margin. Wilde was now throwing lefts and rights to Symonds's head *and* body. Just before the bell, Symonds kept Wilde honest with a cracking right to Jimmy's chin, making his legs buckle.

32 *Mirror of Life* 21 November 1914

From the eighth round through to the 14th, Wilde landed the crisper blows with greater regularity. He made Symonds miss and then scored with sharp counters. Symonds kept coming forward but, as the rounds went by, he found it more and more difficult to land an effective blow.

As the fighters came out for the 15th and final round, most of those watching knew Symonds needed a knockout to win. He tried his heart out in the last three minutes, but Wilde coolly picked him off as he came in.

When the final bell sounded, there was only one winner. An exhausted Symonds smiled ruefully as he and Wilde hugged in the centre of the ring. *Boxing*, *Mirror of Life* and the *Sporting Life* all had Wilde winning every round.

Teddy Lewis had expected Wilde to win and was happy that he had done so. Unfortunately, the odds for a Wilde win had been so short that he had not managed to recoup any of his losses from the recent forfeits he had been forced to pay out to the NSC.

The boxing writers were now firmly of the opinion that Wilde was unbeatable. Symonds had been considered the sternest test of his career so far, yet Wilde had completely outboxed him. The editor of *Mirror of Life* wrote that Wilde 'has no equal at his weight and has beaten men two stones heavier than himself on many occasions. Such performances surpass those of any of the smaller boxers in the history of the ring and what he can accomplish has yet to be discovered'.[33]

33 *Mirror of Life* 28 November 1914

Wilde was now set to fight Tancy Lee for the vacant title in the early part of the new year. In the meantime, Teddy Lewis, along with his associates from the Liverpool Sporting Syndicate, had matched Wilde with former champion Sid Smith.

He was born on 25 February 1889 in Bermondsey, at that time one of south London's poorest areas. In his early teens, Smith started boxing at the Oxford Medical Mission in Abbey Street, Bermondsey.

The Oxford Medical Mission had been set up by John Stansfield, a parish priest and medical practitioner. Its main role was to provide free medical treatment to the destitute. Relying on donations from local philanthropists, Stansfield was soon able to run Bible classes and open a boys' club upstairs.

Stansfield's vision and hope was that the club would give the local street urchins a sense of family belonging. They were encouraged to decorate it, furnish it and keep it tidy. It was here that Smith, along with hundreds of other boys, learned not only how to throw a straight left, but also how to lead a law-abiding, decent life.

Smith was a prodigious talent who relied on his left jab and excellent footwork to outbox his opponents. His earliest recorded fight was in 1907 when he outpointed Curly Osbourne after six rounds in Whitechapel.

By the autumn of 1911, Smith had compiled a 45-4 record and was nominated by the National Sporting Club to fight Stepney's Joe Wilson in the flyweight division's first British title fight.

On 4 December 1911, Smith outpointed Wilson after 20 rounds of sublime boxing. 'His footwork and his defence, along with his brilliant use of the left, was positively superb,' wrote *Boxing* the following week. The one asset Smith lacked was punching power. 'He can land on any opponent pretty much when and where he likes, but his one problem is that his punches can't disturb their peace of mind or serenity of body.'[34]

Buoyed by his success, Smith travelled to America in January 1912, hoping to secure a big-money fight with top-rated bantamweight Johnny Coulon. When the two parties failed to agree terms, Smith returned to London.

On 2 June 1913, Smith defended his British crown against fellow Londoner Bill Ladbury at the Ring, Blackfriars. Ladbury could not lay a glove on Smith during the first six rounds and was made to look like a novice at times as Smith totally outboxed him. Then, in round seven, Ladbury connected with an explosive right that put Smith on the canvas. Smith got up, but he was badly shaken. He was floored a further six times before the end of the round. When the bell went, his cornermen climbed into the ring and carried him back to his stool.

The sudden change of momentum had surprised everyone. Ladbury, sensing victory, was not going to let up. He knocked Smith down again in the ninth and five times in the tenth. By this stage, Smith did not know where he was. Yet, with blood oozing from his mouth, Smith took everything Ladbury could dish out. The crowd cried 'stop it', but the referee let the massacre

34 *Boxing* 9 December 1911

continue. Poor Sid was sent to the canvas eight times in the 11th round before Ladbury finally landed the knockout blow to end the fight.

Smith had taken a terrible beating. After a long and much-needed rest, he returned to the ring and, going into his fight with Wilde, had won four of his last six bouts.

On 3 December 1914, Wilde and Smith put on one of the most skilful exhibitions of boxing that had ever been seen at the Pudsey Street arena in Liverpool.

Both boxed cautiously early on, looking for openings. Wilde caught Smith's jabs with the open palm of his right glove, while Smith neatly slipped Wilde's jabs by moving his head slightly to his left.

The knowledgeable Liverpool crowd watched in wonderment. Of the fourth round, *Boxing* observed that, during those three minutes, 'scientific boxing was at a high-water mark. Smith's cleverness was equal to Jimmy's'.[35]

In the fifth, a solid left to Smith's mid-section made him wince, but he drew applause when he saw Wilde rush at him and made Jimmy fall into the ropes by swaying sideways at the last minute.

Both were working at close quarters by the eighth. Smith scored with an uppercut which knocked Wilde's head back, but Wilde was unmoved and carried on throwing his left and right combinations to Smith's head and body. Unbeknown to everyone except Wilde, that one uppercut from Smith was the turning

35 *Boxing* 9 December 1914

point of the fight. 'He had hit me as hard as he could. I now knew in my mind that he could not knock me out. With that conviction I decided to mix it.'[36]

Up until that point, neither boxer had gained the upper hand. Many watching were fully expecting the fight to go the distance. Wilde had other ideas. 'I feinted for his ribs with my left. Sid dropped his guard to cover and I changed the punch to a right hand to the jaw. I could see the surprise in Sid's eyes, but he had no time to get his glove up. He went down on one knee and was badly shaken. From then on, it was easy.'[37]

Bravely, Smith clambered to his feet. Twice more he was knocked down and twice more he got back up. Wilde drove him to the ropes, where he landed lefts and rights at will until the referee, Frank Bradley, came between them and called off the fight.

The following week, Bradley, writing in *Mirror of Life*, congratulated both Wilde and Smith for their 'masterly skill and clean boxing'.[38]

---

36 Jimmy Wilde *Fighting Was My Business* p.84
37 Ibid p.84
38 *Mirror of Life* 12 December 1914

9
Tancy

BY JANUARY 1915, Wilde was undefeated in 64 reported fights, with 44 of them ending inside the distance. However, it is safe to assume that he had easily taken part in more than 100 contests, as not every boxing show was reported in the newspapers.

If the correct number of fights that Wilde had taken part in was uncertain, the one certainty was that no one had ever seen him beaten.

It was his durability and innate toughness, allied to his marvellous boxing brain, which convinced many boxing observers that Wilde was unbeatable.

Three weeks before his fight with Tancy Lee, the famous referee Eugene Corri called Wilde 'a genius' and said he was 'beyond praise and baffles analysis'.[39]

The sports press had always backed Wilde to win, no matter who he was fighting. Although there was always a tiny doubt in their minds every time he climbed through the ropes as to

39 *Western Mail* 5 January 1915

whether he would be able to overcome the weight advantage his opponent held over him, time and again, normally within five minutes of the fight starting, those same reporters had cast their doubts aside as they sat and watched Wilde completely outclass whoever he was fighting.

The man Wilde was fighting next had worked his way up the fistic ladder and into title contention in a much more understated manner.

James 'Tancy' Lee is one of British boxing's most underrated and most forgotten fighters. Lee was born on 31 January 1882 in Paisley to a Scottish father and an Irish mother. In his early teens, he moved from Paisley to Leith, where he found work as a labourer on the docks. It was a tough, physical job that added strength to an already sinewy, athletic frame.

Soon after starting work, Lee joined a local boxing club and was showing considerable promise, but his boxing career was interrupted when he went to the Boer War in South Africa with the Royal Scots.

By the time he was 20, Lee had returned to Scotland and he carried on with his boxing. Lee's first recorded professional fight was against J. Goodall in February 1906. However, Lee's early professional record is hard to quantify because he was still fighting in the amateurs at the same time.

Simultaneously fighting as an amateur and a professional was strictly against the rules. This led to the one big controversy of Lee's career. In 1910, Lee won the ABA bantamweight championship and received a silver cup worth ten guineas.

On his triumphant return to Leith, a newspaper reporter who recognised Lee informed the chairman of the ABA that he had seen Lee fight in professional bouts. After a short investigation, which proved that the reporter had been correct, Lee was made to hand back the cup and the man he had beaten in the final, Harry Mathias, was given another chance to win the title against William 'Wally' Webb, who had lost to Lee in the quarter-finals.

In the rearranged final, Webb, who had won a bronze medal at the London Olympics two years earlier, outpointed Mathias in a hard-fought contest to win his second ABA crown.

After this regrettable incident, Lee, who had a wife and five children to support, signed with manager Frank Munro, who booked him regular fights at the Victoria Athletic Club in Glasgow and at the Olympia in Edinburgh.

Under the guidance of Munro, Lee made rapid progress in Scotland. His first big win came in March 1914 when he stopped Dan McGrady from Govan in the 12th round to win the Scottish flyweight title.

The impressive win over McGrady persuaded Munro to take Lee down to London to fight Bill Ladbury, who, three months earlier, had lost the British title to Percy Jones.

Fighting in Ladbury's backyard at New Cross Baths, Lee swarmed all over the ex-champion. The boxing writers sitting ringside were surprised. They had fully expected Ladbury to get back to winning ways, but Lee, who had obviously gone under the radar down south, gave Ladbury such a one-sided beating that the referee stopped the fight in the eighth round.

Lee's performance had impressed everyone who had been there to see it, none more so than 'Peggy' Bettinson, who quickly signed up Lee to fight Hanley's Tommy Harrison at the National Sporting Club in a final eliminator for the British title.

On 25 May 1914, one month after beating Ladbury, Lee outworked and outmuscled the man from the Potteries and was a clear winner after ten rounds.

Tancy Lee was now set to fight the greatest little man of his age.

Early in the new year, Wilde, Baillieu and sparring partners Dai Mathews and Len Rowlands made their way to their training headquarters in Porthcawl. This time their base was the Pier Hotel. The Esplanade, where Wilde had stayed while preparing to meet Joe Symonds, was now being used to house newly recruited soldiers.

The Sportsman reported how Porthcawl had changed in the six weeks since they had last been there. 'War fever has taken a firm grip on the place. Its population has increased by 3,000, mainly recruits to the Glamorgan Bantams. Part of the drill grounds are in front of the Pier Hotel, where a thousand-odd patriots are being put through their paces.'[40]

The decision to go to Porthcawl, as before, did not sit comfortably with Jimmy or Elizabeth. Once again, Wilde was away from his beloved wife and young son – not to mention Elizabeth's cooking. Elizabeth and David were allowed, on Baillieu's instruction, to visit once a week. This only made Wilde's

40 *The Sportsman* 14 January 1915

yearning for home even stronger. Luckily, Mathews, Rowlands and Percy Jones kept his spirits up.

Back in Pontypridd, Teddy Lewis had so much confidence in his man that he had already arranged for Wilde to fight in Liverpool against Glasgow's Johnny Best just 24 days after the Lee fight.

Wilde had been fighting so often that it was a case of simply ticking over in Porthcawl. To Wilde's great relief, his hand was not giving him any trouble. Even so, Jimmy found Baillieu 'stricter on some points of training than I felt was necessary'.[41]

A week before the fight, Baillieu was confined to bed with influenza. Wilde carried on training as normal, with Baillieu popping down to see him every now and again when he could summon enough strength.

The boxing writers visited Wilde's training headquarters and, after watching him work out, noted how well he looked. They left Porthcawl convinced that Wilde would be taking the Lonsdale belt back to Wales.

What the writers had not been privvy to was how unhappy Jimmy felt at his seaside training base. Then, four days before the fight on the Thursday morning, Wilde woke up with a fever and a runny nose.

Within 24 hours, Wilde's symptoms had worsened and he was unable to train, so he stayed in bed. He was expecting Elizabeth to come down to see him that morning, but there was no sign of her. Jimmy waited in his room.

---

41 Jimmy Wilde *Fighting Was My Business* p.89

By late afternoon, Wilde, who had a temperature and felt weak, was growing more and more concerned about the whereabouts of his wife. He was worried she had been in an accident on her way from Tylorstown. He became so anxious that he threatened to leave the confines of his room and find out for himself.

Shortly after Jimmy made his intentions known, Elizabeth, to his great relief, burst into his room. She was flushed with rage. 'She had been waiting around for hours,' Jimmy recounted. 'Baillieu and his wife had told her that I had gone out because they knew what she would say when she found me as ill as I was just three days before a fight. Elizabeth eventually left with tears in her eyes, vowing vengeance on Baillieu.'[42]

On her return to Tylorstown, Elizabeth wasted little time in visiting Teddy Lewis and informing him of Jimmy's condition and the lack of care shown by Baillieu.

Lewis begged Wilde to pull out of the fight. A note from the doctor would end the matter. The fight could easily be rescheduled. Wilde, however, was determined to go through with it. He felt that, if he postponed the fight, he would be letting everyone down.

Elizabeth pleaded with him to change his mind. She used every possible trick she could think of in an attempt to persuade him to cancel the fight, telling him that all those hard-working men in Tylorstown who had backed him with their hard-earned money were now going to lose every penny because, unbeknown to them, he was going into the ring unfit to fight.

---

42 Jimmy Wilde *Fighting Was My Business* p.90

Eventually, Elizabeth and Teddy had to accept the fact that Jimmy had made up his mind and was not going to follow their advice.

The big fight was proving to be a big distraction from the war. On the day of the fight, 25 January 1915, the *Sporting Life* carried a front page preview of that evening's contest. However, a report describing how Britain had won the Battle of Dogger Bank in the North Sea by sinking German cruisers dominated the front page. In another column, readers were urged to send tobacco and cigarettes to the troops on the Front.

The front page of the *Western Mail* was equally sombre, reporting that later that night, when Wilde and Lee were battling it out in the ring, large crowds were expected in Cardiff to welcome back 129 sick and wounded soldiers when they returned to Cardiff on a hospital train.

Shortly before 2pm on the afternoon of the fight, 'Peggy' Bettinson called both men to the scales at the NSC. Lee, who had trained in Portobello on the Edinburgh coast, looked hard and lean. He weighed 1lb inside the flyweight limit. Wilde, who looked pale and drawn, was muffled up in a heavy coat, scarf and trilby. He stepped on to the scales fully clothed and weighed 6st 12lb. Wilde's main thought was to get back to his room for a lie-down.

Wilde, Baillieu and Lewis had done their best to keep Wilde's condition secret, but it must have been obvious to Bettinson and all the officials in attendance at the weigh-in that Wilde was seriously under the weather. Even so, he was still a 2/1 favourite with the bookies.

As the time for battle grew near, Wilde could not stop shivering in his dressing room. Before all his previous fights, Wilde, Lewis, Driscoll and assistant David Hughes had always been upbeat, relaxed and confident. Now, his body racked with influenza, the mood was one of resignation.

At 10pm, Tancy Lee was the first to climb into the ring with his trainer Alf Denhart. Wilde arrived moments later. As the master of ceremonies introduced the boxers through his loud hailer, Wilde wondered 'whether I could lift my arms to even start a pretence of fighting'.[43]

Before Wilde had time to have another thought, the bell had clanged and the fight was on. Wilde threw a tentative left jab. Lee replied with a jab of his own, then both men fell into a clinch. Lee walked Wilde back to the ropes. Lee hit Wilde on the back of the neck as Wilde bent over, which forced him to touch the canvas momentarily. On resumption, Lee kept Wilde at close quarters and forced the pace with two-handed combinations.

Lee was intent on denying Wilde any space in which to get his punches off, attaching himself to Wilde like a magnet while he flailed away to Jimmy's head and body.

Boxing vividly described the bout as being 'fought out in earnest monotone. There were neither thrills nor spills. Lee was as hard as his native granite and he hustled Wilde all over the ring.'[44]

By the fifth round, the odds on a Wilde victory had lengthened from 2/1 to even money. Lee's extra weight in the clinches was taking its toll. The NSC crowd was surprised that the referee did not

43 Jimmy Wilde *Fighting Was My Business* p.92
44 *Boxing* 30 January 1915

admonish Tancy for his constant rabbit punching. Many at ringside thought that, if Lee had thrown more legal blows and refrained from throwing illegitimate ones, he would have stopped Wilde earlier.

For the next six rounds, the fight progressed in the same manner. Wilde, with his back pinned to the ropes, tried his best to duck and dodge the lefts and rights that Lee constantly threw at him.

A fine uppercut which missed Lee by inches could have changed Wilde's fortunes in the 14th. The Scotsman demonstrated his extra strength by pushing Wilde backwards to the ropes where Lee, who leant all his weight on Wilde, bundled him through the ropes. Thankfully, Wilde managed to scramble back into the ring in time. 'Sheer doggedness was my only advantage in this fight,' he would later remember.[45]

In the 15th, Wilde's left ear had become swollen and disfigured from Lee's rights hands. His corner were growing more and more concerned with every passing round. As Jimmy weakened, Tancy got stronger.

The man from Leith had got his tactics spot on. He had not given Wilde enough space to punch and had tired him out by bearing his extra weight on him in the clinches.

In the 17th round, with Wilde taking a battering on the ropes, his cornermen jumped into the ring waving a white towel. The fight was over.

Wilde had taken a pummelling. His lips were cut, his head was throbbing and he had a cauliflower ear. As Lee was

45 Jimmy Wilde *Fighting Was My Business* p.92

announced the winner, Wilde was 'not alert enough to be sorry that I had lost'.[46]

Teddy's main concern was to get Wilde back up to his room at the NSC as quickly as possible. Once there, Teddy tried to reduce the swelling on Wilde's ear by lancing it. Wilde, who was semi-conscious, just wanted to see Elizabeth, who had not been allowed into the NSC because it was a male-only club.

Ralph Lisle, who had refereed many of Wilde's fights, went to Elizabeth's hotel nearby. Eventually he managed to find her room and they both made their way back to the NSC. Lisle persuaded Bettinson to waive the rules and let Elizabeth stay with her husband. Bettinson, who admired Wilde greatly, relented.

As the new holder of the Lonsdale belt, Tancy Lee, and not Jimmy Wilde, would now be doing the rounds of the music halls in the coming weeks. As the new champion, Tancy would be the one who would be invited to theatres, along with his belt, where his fight with Wilde would be reshown all over the land to a rapt audience.

For Jimmy Wilde, a long rest and time to heal were the order of the day.

46 Ibid p.93

10

Comeback

ON HIS return to Tylorstown, Wilde was given a warm reception. It was good to be back home with his wife and young son. *Boxing* dramatically summed up the mood after Wilde's defeat by writing that 'all of Wales is now grovelling in the dust and ashes of desolation'.[47]

Far from wallowing in self pity, the Welsh contingent and members of the National Sporting Club, in particular, were incensed at how Lee had repeatedly rabbit punched Wilde throughout the fight and how lenient the referee, John Herbert Douglas, had been with the Scotsman.

Wilde was philosophical about his first defeat. He knew he should have listened to Elizabeth and Teddy and pulled out of the fight. Having the flu had robbed him of all his strength, but he wanted everyone to know that 'on the night, Tancy had deserved his victory'.[48]

Wilde was annoyed when reports emerged revealing he had been unfit to fight. It is a mark of the man that he did not want

47 *Boxing* 30 January 1915
48 Jimmy Wilde *Fighting Was My Business* p.94

Tancy's victory to be tarnished in any way and he was always uncomfortable when people attributed the loss to him being ill.

Wilde still believed that, when fully fit, he could beat Tancy. Teddy Lewis was of the same opinion. 'I will back Jimmy against Lee for £500 at 7st 12lb ringside,' he told *Mirror of Life,* adding that 'Jimmy suffered a lot against Lee, but we were splendidly treated at the NSC and we can never really repay the kindness of Mr Bettinson and the club.'[49]

While Jimmy was recuperating, he and Elizabeth decided that Baillieu's services would no longer be required. Benny Williams, a local man who had been a good sprinter in his youth, had admired Wilde for some time and was more than happy to assist him. More importantly, Wilde and Williams got on well from the very beginning. 'Elizabeth liked Benny, who was a small, downright man and well known in boxing circles. Unlike Baillieu, Benny led a man into training, whereas Baillieu and a great many others were inclined to drive.'[50]

From now on, all training would be done in Tylorstown. What is more, Wilde had found a new hobby. Bombardier Billy Wells, the British heavyweight champion, had recommended that Jimmy take up golf. 'The fresh air and the exercise will do you the power of good,' Billy had told him. Wilde took to golf like a fish to water and, within a few weeks, was playing up to three rounds a day on the course at Cwmbach.

On 25 March 1915, after exactly two months out of the ring, Wilde returned to action against Sid Shields, a tough battler

49 *Mirror of Life* 6 February 1915
50 Jimmy Wilde *Fighting Was My Business* p.96

from Glasgow who had recently been stopped in the 15th round by Joe Symonds.

It was an astute business decision by the Liverpool Sporting Syndicate to stage the show on the eve of the Grand National. Having Wilde on the bill was always a guarantee that another one or two thousand would be put on the gate, but, with Liverpool already full of racegoers, the Pudsey Street arena was full to capacity on the night of the fight.

Inside the arena, the Irish King's Liverpool Regiment took the opportunity to recruit as many young men as they possibly could. A captain from the regiment stood in the centre of the ring and told the crowd that 'we are getting no further on and only by having more numbers can we make progress'.[51]

Shields, it seemed, thought his best chance of victory was to end the fight early. His rushing tactics took Wilde by surprise at first and he was bundled over without taking a punch early in the opening round. However, he then managed to subdue Shields with his left jab.

Shields came out in the same vein in the second. Wilde slipped most of his jabs and scored with his own. Two minutes into the round, Wilde caught Shields with a tremendous right on the jaw and put him down. Shields got up on unsteady legs at the count of nine, but Wilde was on him like a flash. Another right put Shields down again in exactly the same spot as the first knockdown. Shields got up, but he had no time to get out of harm's way. A thudding left to the body and a follow-up right to the side of the head sent him down and out.

---

51 *Manchester Sporting Chronicle* 26 March 1915

The jubilant crowd clapped and cheered as the master of ceremonies announced Wilde as the winner. Liverpool, which had a large population of Welsh migrants who 30 years earlier had travelled north to build houses and work on the docks, was like a second home to Jimmy. What made his victory over Shields even sweeter was the fact that he had beaten him much quicker than Symonds had done.

In April 1915, while training for his upcoming fight against Dido Gains, Wilde started to experience stomach pains. At first, Wilde thought it was just one of those niggles that every fighter gets. However, as time went on, the pain became more intense. Within a couple of weeks of it starting, Wilde was in agony and unable to train at all on some days.

Teddy Lewis suggested Wilde see a specialist in London. After numerous examinations, it was initially thought he had appendicitis and would need surgery, but the specialist eventually assured him an operation would not be necessary after all and that the condition would clear up with a prolonged period of rest.

After six weeks of taking it easy, Wilde was looking and feeling a lot better. His well-being was given a further boost at the end of May when he was the cornerman for stablemate Llew Edwards, who was challenging Birmingham's Owen Moran for the British featherweight title. Moran was disqualified for persistently throwing low blows in the tenth round, which meant that Teddy Lewis had now managed two British champions in Percy Jones and Edwards. His main aim now was to add Jimmy Wilde to that roll of honour.

With his strength restored, Wilde resumed light training. One of his greatest joys was taking part in exhibition matches to raise money for the war effort or for a recently retired boxer. Wilde was always given a warm reception and delighted the large crowds with a show of his skills against a whole host of soldiers from different regiments.

The charity shows were not only a way for Wilde to improve his wind in the ring, they were also great social occasions. Men who were amateur boxers in the forces got the chance to spar three rounds with the best boxers in Britain. It was an experience they would never have again and one they would remember for the rest of their lives. These exhibitions, which often attracted crowds of 5,000 or more, not only boosted morale, but served as ideal places to recruit new soldiers.

On 24 July 1915, Wilde took on Driver Benthew, a novice boxer who was serving with the Royal Fleet Auxiliary. It soon became apparent to the 6,000 people who had turned up at the Pheasant Inn Grounds in Carbrook, near Sheffield, that Benthew should not have been in the ring with a fighter of Wilde's ability.

Concentrating on Benthew's ample mid-section, Wilde floored him in the third and fourth before Benthew turned away in surrender in the fifth. For Wilde, who had not had a serious contest for two months, it was the easiest of returns.

The boxing in Carbrook had been so well attended that Wilde returned there three weeks later. Although there was a healthy turnout, wet weather restricted the attendance. Those who were there saw Wilde at his brilliant best. His opponent,

Bermondsey's George Clark, was like a rabbit in the headlights. Wilde's combination punching was mesmerising and, after taking a real shellacking for nigh-on 23 minutes, he was retired by his corner in the eighth round.

On 23 September 1915, the Liverpool Sports Syndicate staged a three-fight Wales versus Scotland card. Wilde fought Walter Buchan, a stablemate and sparring partner of Tancy Lee.

Buchan, who had an extensive amateur career before turning professional, was a stylish stand-up boxer. Lee, who had helped Buchan in his preparations for the fight, told *Boxing* he would not be surprised if Buchan sprang an upset.

In the opening round, both boxers carefully sparred for openings. Both received applause as they neatly evaded each other's jabs and attempted to score with counter-punches.

In the second and third, Wilde drew Buchan in by feinting and would then land sharp lefts and rights. By the fourth round, it seemed as though Wilde had sussed out the Glasgow man. He went after Buchan and there was now more devil in his punches. Buchan was starting to wilt under the pressure Wilde was putting him under. That pressure told in the fifth. Non-stop lefts and rights to the Scotsman's head and body forced Buchan to half turn away. Wilde immediately stopped punching as Buchan held up his left glove to signal that he had had enough.

The roof nearly came off the arena as the crowd cheered. It had been a pleasing fight to watch while it had lasted. The Pudsey Street faithful had seen textbook boxing by both men, rapid combination punching from Wilde and grit and courage from Buchan. What is more, Wales had won the international two-nil. Earlier in the evening, Tylorstown's Sam Coombes beat Glasgow's Johnny Campbell and the third bout, between Jack Conn, who was also from Tylorstown, and Walter Buchan's brother, Robert, ended in a draw.

Meanwhile, Joe Symonds had worked his way into a position to challenge Tancy Lee for the British title. In the 11 months that had passed since he lost to Wilde, Symonds had won 12 fights in a row, with seven of them ending before the final bell.

The most spectacular of those wins came against Bill Ladbury in March. The crowd had hardly settled into their seats before the fight was over. Symonds knocked out Ladbury with his first punch after just 22 seconds. When they fought again in June, poor Ladbury managed to last just one round longer. Wins over top contenders Dido Gains, Johnny Hughes, Sid Smith and Johnny Best firmly placed Symonds in the No. 1 contender slot for Lee's crown.

On 18 October 1915, Tancy Lee, a 3/1 on favourite, lost his British title to Joe Symonds in the 16th round. Although the Plymouth man was 12 years Tancy's junior, he was not given much of a chance. However, he never gave Tancy the opportunity to manhandle him. Boxing beautifully behind his left jab, Symonds showed those at the NSC the perfect way to 'mill on the retreat'.

Wilde and Lewis, who had watched the fight from ringside, quickly made their way from London back to Wales because they had a ferry to catch. They were off to Dublin, via Holyhead, for Jimmy's fight against bantamweight Peter Cullen.

Irish promoter J.J. O'Neil had recently purchased the 2,000-seat Drill Hall in North Brunswick Street in the hope that the venue would breathe new life into boxing in Dublin.

Having Wilde at the top of the bill was a masterstroke by O'Neil. Every ticket was sold and, on the night of the fight, more than 100 fans without tickets were turned away at the door.

Cullen, who was returning to the ring after a long lay-off, had weighed in at 8st 6lb earlier that afternoon, a full 2st heavier than Wilde. However, the Irishman's extra weight was no advantage to him whatsoever. Wilde was sublime. He knocked Cullen over in the second and handed out a steady beating for the next seven rounds. Most of those watching did not think Cullen would last as long as he did, but he showed an amazing ability to take heavy shots until his corner finally rescued him near the end of the ninth.

Although the crossing had been rough, Jimmy had avoided seasickness. He and Teddy had a bet at Holyhead to see who would be able to last the longest without throwing up as they crossed the Irish Sea. When they arrived back in Holyhead, the bet was void. Jimmy and Teddy had both felt queasy during the journey, but neither was prepared to let on. Only when they got back on *terra firma* and were on their way back to Tylorstown did they both laugh and admit to each other how close they had come to being ill. The Irish Sea in late October had given Wilde more trouble than Cullen had done in the ring.

Wilde then re-trod old ground. On 27 November, he faced Tommy Hughes, who he had beaten two years earlier in seven rounds, at the Palace Theatre in Barrow. This time, Hughes, who was on the defensive and shipping punishment throughout, lasted one round longer before he was retired by his corner.

The *North Western Daily Mail* reporter was impressed with what they saw. 'Wilde is a wonder,' the correspondent wrote. 'He is the most marvellous piece of fighting machinery seen in the ring. One hardly knows what to admire most; the dazzling rapidity of his blows or the extraordinary way in which he ducked and avoided the blows from his opponent. On present form he will be a big favourite against Symonds.'[52]

It seems inconceivable to think nowadays that a boxer would have three fights in a span of 11 days, but that is what Wilde did in the last month of 1915.

The first of these was against the tremendously experienced Glaswegian Johnny Best, a fighter who had shared a ring with everyone of note in the flyweight and bantamweight divisions.

Best, who had started his career in 1910, was a tough but light-punching boxer who had been stopped by Tancy Lee in the 17th round in 1913 but had then gone on to outpoint Alf Mansfield, Johnny Hughes, Dan McGrady and Sid Shields. In 1915, Best had fought two draws with Sid Smith and been stopped in the 11th by Joe Symonds. Coming into his fight with Wilde, Best had recently fought a ten-round draw with Dido Gains in Coventry.

Although Best came into the ring weighing 8st 4lb, it was Wilde who had the heavier punch. As early as the first minute, Wilde's jab had Best on the retreat. Best was simply overwhelmed

52 *North Western Daily Mail* 28 November 1915

by Wilde's fast combinations. Floored in the fifth and in the ninth, Best took a frightful beating until the 14th round when, after being knocked down for the third time in the fight, the referee, Jack Thwaites, stopped the bout.

Four days later, Wilde travelled from Liverpool, where he had fought Best, to Bradford in west Yorkshire where he knocked out the woefully overmatched Danny Elliott in two rounds at the Central Baths.

A return match with Sid Smith at the National Sporting Club on 20 December capped off an extremely busy period for Wilde. Smith, who had taken the fight on the agreement that he weigh no more than 8st 2lb on the afternoon of the fight, weighed in half a pound over the agreed limit and had to do some vigorous skipping wearing a couple of thick, woolly pullovers to sweat off the weight.

Wilde was all over Smith like a threshing machine from the first bell. Lefts and rights from Wilde thudded into Smith's head and body. The man from Bermondsey was knocked down three times in the fifth and once in the sixth. In the seventh, Wilde floored him twice more. Smith just could not cope with Wilde's non-stop attacks and went down on one knee near the end of the round simply to have some respite from it all until the bell rang. Smith was knocked down three times in the eighth, which prompted the referee to stop the fight.

'Peggy' Bettinson gave Wilde the best Christmas present he had ever had when he announced that he would be fighting Symonds for the title early in the new year.

The war had now been raging for 17 months and, knowing that many of his contemporaries had joined the forces, Wilde felt compelled to do so himself. After taking part in an exhibition to raise money for the military in Birmingham, Wilde presented himself to the local recruiting office before catching the train home. After a thorough medical examination, Wilde was taken aback when the recruiting officer called him back into his office to tell him he had been rejected due to having a weak leg. The *Porthcawl News* reported that 'this will astonish all those who have seen Wilde in the ring'.[53]

When he left Birmingham that day, little did Wilde know how much angst failing that medical would cause him in the coming months.

As well as appearing in exhibitions to raise money for the War Fund, Wilde prepared for his meeting with Joe Symonds by fighting three times in 19 days. It is a schedule that would be unheard of, and not allowed, today.

The first of those three fights was against Billy Rowlands from Porthcawl, who was knocked out in seven rounds at the Empire Theatre in Swansea on 8 January 1916. After the fight, Jimmy's gloves were sold at auction for five guineas.

Just over a fortnight later, Wilde fought Bermondsey battler Tommy Noble at New Cross Baths. Noble had only been a professional for 11 months when he fought Wilde, but he had already built up a 23-3-3 record, mainly fighting at the Ring in Blackfriars.

53 *Porthcawl News* 15 January 1915

New Cross Baths was full to capacity when Wilde and Noble climbed through the ropes on the evening of 24 January. Although many in the crowd were rooting for local man Noble, just as many had come to see Wilde.

The opening two rounds were cagey, with both fighters carefully sparring for openings. In the third, the pace quickened and Noble suffered a cut above his left eye from one of Wilde's slashing rights. By the fifth round, Wilde was scoring at will with lightning-fast four-punch salvos that bewildered Noble at times, but the 18-year-old gathered himself and fired back, drawing blood from Wilde's nose.

The pace of the bout caused both men to take a breather in an uneventful sixth, but Wilde got his second wind in the seventh, hurting Noble with a left to the mouth and rights to the body which made the Londoner clinch.

Noble's eye continued to bleed freely in the eighth and ninth. Despite scoring with a good right to Wilde's chin in the tenth, it was becoming obvious to those watching that Noble was starting to feel the pace.

The end came suddenly in the 11th. Noble missed with a swinging right and, as his momentum carried him forwards, Wilde threw a perfectly timed left uppercut which dropped Noble on to his hands and knees. Noble shook his head, trying to regain his senses. Bravely, he rose at the count of seven but, unbeknown to him, his corner had already thrown in the towel while the referee was counting.

Three days later, Wilde capped off his prearations for the Symonds fight by knocking out the vastly overmatched Jimmy

Morton in two rounds at Pudsey Street. The Liverpool faithful wished Wilde well as he left the ring. They were certain that the next time they saw him they would be watching the newly crowned British champion.

11
The Lonsdale Belt At Last

WHEN JIMMY told Elizabeth that Teddy Lewis had arranged for him to fight Joe Symonds for the British title, she was as happy as he was. 'Now they will see the real Jimmy Wilde,' she told him. Elizabeth knew that a fit and healthy Jimmy was virtually unbeatable.[54]

For Wilde, it was a chance to repay the faith shown in him by Lewis and Bettinson since that miserable night against Tancy Lee. When Wilde was in the ring fighting, *he* was in control. But when he was at home, fears and doubts ran through his mind during quiet periods. It was the constant support he received from Elizabeth that kept him believing and striving for the title.

Wilde was a happy man at the start of 1916. Not only was Elizabeth expecting their second child (their son Verdun would be born on 16 March) but, in Benny Williams, Wilde had found the perfect trainer and adviser. 'Living at home and training with Benny Williams, I approached my second bid

54 Jimmy Wilde *Fighting Was My Business* p.98

for the championship in a very different frame of mind. That nightmare period at Porthcawl seemed far away.'[55]

Putting Wilde through his paces were sparring partners Billy Jones, Ivor Day, Jim Evans and Walter Rossi. Wilde was giving away anything up to 20lb in weight to each man, but he never let up in sparring, giving as good as he got as he sparred three rounds with each man every day.

Jones, Day, Evans and Rossi were all tough fighters who never complained. If Wilde had given them a hard time the day before, they turned up the following day expecting the same. It was a tough way to earn a living, but everyone in the gym had a good attitude and the atmosphere was light and upbeat.

Meanwhile, Symonds was training on the south coast at Paignton in Devon. It was an invigorating location, especially in early February.

Since winning the title from Tancy Lee in October, Symonds had been as active as Wilde had been. He had fought twice in November, beating Johnny Gratton with a third-round knockout and Johnny Hughes on points after 15 rounds. He also fought twice in December, being disqualified against Sam Keller for a low blow and then, curiously, finding himself on the other side of a disqualification against former British bantamweight champion George 'Digger' Stanley, who was slung out by referee Eugene Corri for hitting low and for headbutting Symonds in a clinch.

On 7 February, just one week before fighting Wilde, Symonds knocked out George Dando in the first round. All

55 Ibid p.98

of Symonds's last five fights had been contested at the 8st limit, so his title was never at stake. Even so, taking a fight just seven days before a British title defence was a considerable risk and would not be allowed to happen nowadays.

In the week before the fight, all the boxing scribes believed Wilde would be the winner. Wilde had already outpointed Symonds 15 months earlier and they were unanimously of the opinion that the return contest would go the same way.

On the afternoon of 14 February 1916, both men weighed in at the National Sporting Club. It was the first time a weigh-in had ever been filmed. Wilde was first to step on to the scales and weighed 6st 11lb fully clothed. In a spot of gamesmanship, Symonds also stepped on to the scales fully clothed. Bettinson was not impressed and told Symonds to strip to his underpants. Symonds did so and weighed 7st 13lb.

Wilde looked a picture of health at the weigh-in. He smiled and waved to the crowd and looked extremely relaxed. 'I knew his power and I knew my own. Frankly, it did not occur to me that I could lose. The only question I asked myself was how long would it take me to win.'[56]

This confidence was not arrogance or misplaced belief. On the contrary, it was due to the fact Wilde had beaten Symonds once before and had studied him at ringside since they had last fought. Wilde's gameplan was to wait for Symonds to lead, make him miss and then score with counter-punches.

56 Jimmy Wilde *Fighting Was My Business* p.100

Bookmakers believed Wilde would be the victor. Earlier in the week, Wilde had been a 2/1 on favourite. By the time of the fight, the odds had shortened to 7/4 on. Symonds was 7/4 against. There were few takers for the Plymouth man.

At 9.40pm, the extra-bright lights provided by the *Daily Mirror* were switched on and given a few minutes to warm up. Symonds was the first into the ring with his trainer Joe Smith, Owen Moran and Sam Friend. Wilde quickly followed accompanied by Benny Williams, Jim Driscoll and Billy Baxter.

After introducing both boxers, Bettinson gave Wilde and Symonds their final instructions. As Wilde and Symonds stood in their respective corners waiting for the bell, the din of chatter faded and silence descended on the room.

Symonds threw the first punch of the fight, a straight left to Wilde's face, and it was clear during the first couple of minutes of the opening round that Symonds had decided to be the aggressor. Wilde deftly shuffled sideways and backwards, making Symonds fall short, then swiftly countered with fast straight lefts.

Symonds had adopted an unusual trait when he was fighting. He had a habit of leaping into his opponent with both feet off the canvas while simultaneously throwing a left hook. Wilde, who had seen Symonds do this before, would either block the punch with his right glove or duck underneath it, take half a step back and then land his own left.

The fight was fast paced, with Symonds constantly coming forward. Wilde was content to box within himself and counter. Although there was a lot of feinting and missing, both scored with left jabs and, when the chance presented itself, the occasional right. Symonds, however, was shading the early rounds with his greater workrate.

In the fifth, Symonds drove Wilde backwards to the ropes with a two-fisted barrage which Wilde cleverly evaded by bobbing, weaving and ducking. Symonds never stopped throwing punches for the entire three minutes.

The sixth was Wilde's best round so far. The exertion of the previous round had taken a lot out of Symonds. Sensing that his opponent needed to take a breather, Wilde forced Symonds back for the first time in the fight with a tirade of lefts and rights to head and body.

By the eighth round, Wilde had a slight swelling under his right eye, while the right side of Symonds's face was reddened from Wilde's left jabs. Wilde started to score with his left uppercut, which lifted Symonds's head up and back, and he started to thud home right hands to the side of Joe's head.

In the ninth, Symonds was still the aggressor. However, unlike in the early rounds, Wilde was now replying with left and right combinations. Wilde's defence was sublime. He effortlessly slipped Symonds's wild swings and then replied with stinging left jabs to the face. As all fighters know, missing makes you tire quicker than anything, and Symonds was missing a great deal.

In the tenth, Wilde sensed this and went after Symonds like never before. 'Jimmy's left flashed out like a lizard's tongue. He followed with rapid rights to the face. Jimmy slipped, only to rise and pepper his man unmercifully. For a time, it looked as if Wilde had the full measure of his man. He seemed to think so himself and was wide open to a terrific left hook on the gong which must have shaken him to his toes.'[57]

That heavy left hook had made Wilde realise that Symonds was still a great threat and that he could take nothing for granted. Wilde was still dazed during the early stages of the 11th but, by the second half of the round, his head had cleared and he opened up on Symonds again. Lefts and rights forced Symonds to give ground. Gallantly, Symonds fired back with both fists but, whereas Wilde's punches had landed, the vast majority of Symonds's fell short.

Wilde was biding his time. His opportunity came in the 12th. Symonds left himself open to a left hook, taking it flush on the jaw. Badly shaken, Symonds tottered backwards into a neutral corner, standing upright with his arms down by his sides. Wilde fired 16 unanswered lefts and rights to the jaw, knocking Symonds's head from side to side. Symonds, in an effort to avoid the avalanche of blows, doubled over. Wilde threw two vicious rights to the left side of Symonds's body, forcing him to go down on one knee, his left glove held out in a gesture of surrender. Just as Symonds's knee had touched the canvas, the referee, J.H.T. Douglas, had climbed on to the side of the ring to officially end the fight.

Symonds, a true sportsman, immediately walked over on unsteady legs to Wilde and shook his right glove before wearily making his way back to his corner.

---

57 *Boxing* 16 February 1916

Wilde sat in his corner with his head momentarily bowed, the meaning of his victory sinking in. Jim Driscoll lifted him off his stool and Teddy Lewis, beaming with joy, climbed into the ring to join in the celebrations. Many years later, Wilde would recall: 'To tell the truth, I have never felt so gloriously happy. Many championship fights ended my way afterwards, but the first was incomparable.'[58]

58 Jimmy Wilde *Fighting Was My Business* p.101

12

The Mystery Of Johnny Rosner

THE DAY after his victory over Joe Symonds, 'Peggy' Bettinson presented Wilde with the Lord Lonsdale challenge belt in a function room at the National Sporting Club. As the gleaming belt was placed around Wilde's slender waist, the Welsh members spontaneously gave a stirring rendition of 'Land Of My Fathers', which was followed by loud and prolonged applause. A battered and bruised Symonds shook hands with Wilde. They briefly discussed how tough the fight had been and wished each other the best of luck for the future before parting ways.

For Symonds, it would be his last fight at 8st. He had already made up his mind that, from now on, he would campaign as a bantamweight.[59]

Wilde, as was the norm, had little time to rest on his laurels after returning home to a hero's welcome in Tylorstown. Teddy Lewis already had a fight set up for him against Sam Keller on 9 March at the West London Stadium in Marylebone.

---

59 Symonds went on to make two unsuccessful challenges for the British bantamweight title, losing to Joe Fox in 1917 and Tommy Noble the following year. He retired in 1924 and became a referee. He died in Plymouth in 1953, aged 58.

Keller, a clever boxer from Aldgate, was one of the most experienced fighters Wilde had ever shared a ring with. It is thought he started boxing in 1902 at the age of 16, with most of his early fights staged at the Wonderland arena in Whitechapel. In 1907, he had a spell in America where he fought 'no decision' bouts against local fighters in New York and Philadelphia. On his return to England, Keller fought for anyone willing to hire his services.

Although he had lost to Bill Ladbury, Percy Jones, Sid Smith and Joe Symonds, Keller was more often than not still standing at the final bell. However, he was regarded as a 'marking time' opponent for the top men in the division.

Boxing, who quite rightly considered Keller to be a couple of notches below Wilde in class, was not sold on the match. Such was the confidence in the Wilde camp that, when Keller weighed in one pound over the agreed limit of 8st 3lb, Wilde and Lewis were more than willing to let it go and concede the weight rather than insist on Keller sweating it off.

The Aldgate man started off confidently, using all his experience and craftiness to navigate the opening three rounds without too much bother. That all changed in the fourth when Wilde jabbed Keller in the face 14 consecutive times without reply. It was an act of ring wizardry that stunned the rapt audience.

That one piece of magic made poor Keller go into a defensive shell. From the fifth round onwards, Keller became a human heavy bag. Wilde dominated the next three rounds, jabbing and scoring at will with his right. Towards the end of the eighth round, Keller's corner had seen enough and threw in the towel.

Frank Bradley, who, as well as being a referee, was the editor of *Mirror of Life*, was perplexed when it was announced that Wilde's next fight would be against Sid Smith at Hoxton Baths on 27 March. 'When Wilde and Smith met at Liverpool I had the pleasure of refereeing and, although Smith was slightly ahead, when I intervened his chances were hopeless,' Bradley wrote in his editorial. 'When a return took place last December, Wilde won most convincingly and I fail to see the necessity for a third match.'[60]

Bradley was right to be sceptical. Even though he came into the Wilde fight after outpointing Sid Shields a month before, Smith was definitely on the slide. The only justification for the contest was that it provided Smith with a decent payday.

Despite the air of pessimism surrounding Smith's chances, Wilde was not underestimating the former champion. He let Smith do most of the leading in the opening round, slipping and ducking out of danger as Smith came forward. Had the fight been at the National Sporting Club, the level of skill on show would have drawn gasps of appreciation. At Hoxton Baths, however, it drew a certain amount of derision. They had paid to see a toe-to-toe tear-up, not scientific boxing.

The crowd's reaction seemed to stir Wilde. He upped the pace significantly in the latter half of the first, flooring Smith twice, the first knockdown coming from a right to the chest, the second from a right to the jaw.

60 *Mirror of Life* 25 March 1916

Wilde was intent on getting the fight over with as quickly as possible. The end came in the third when Wilde drove Smith to the ropes with a series of lefts and rights. Slowly, the London veteran, who was overwhelmed by the volume of punches coming his way, sank to his hands and knees and was counted out.

For Wilde, life as a challenger had been busy. Now he was the champion, he was in demand even more. As well as taking part in countless exhibitions at military camps to raise money for the troops, Wilde returned to Jack Scarrott's booth to make one memorable guest appearance.

What took place at the fairground at Tredegar that afternoon has since passed into boxing folklore. Scarrott asked Jimmy if he would be willing to do a one-off stint on his booth, taking on all-comers for £40. Wilde, who found it hard to say 'no' to anybody, let alone his old mentor Scarrott, agreed.

Legend has it that Wilde boxed for three-and-a-half hours straight, knocking out 19 men. Then, after a 30-minute break, Wilde returned to knock out four more. Twenty-three men knocked out in four hours. To this day, this amazing feat is still one of Welsh boxing's most enduring and often-told stories when Wilde's name is brought up in conversation.

Now that he was the proud holder of the Lonsdale belt, Wilde's goal was to defend it twice more at the National Sporting Club so that the belt would be his to keep. The boxing writers, as well as Teddy Lewis, were struggling to find suitable contenders.

The most creditable was Tancy Lee. The only problem was that Lee was now fighting at 8st 4lb. Would Tancy be able to boil his 34-year-old body down to 8st without weakening himself to such an extent that it would compromise the quality of his performance?

With few serious challengers in Britain, Lewis spoke to Jim Harris, the general manager of the Pudsey Street stadium. Harris proposed pitting Wilde against an American.

Lewis liked the idea. Having Wilde fight an American would be a sell-out for certain.

Harris telegraphed fight agent Dan McKettrick in New York. McKettrick represented a fighter named 'Young' Johnny Rosner, a 20-year-old from Brooklyn who had held his own with bantamweights, mostly in 'no decision' bouts, even though he had never weighed more than 7st 10lb.

Rosner arrived in London on 27 March 1916 after a ten-day journey across the Atlantic. Rosner's two managers, Dan McKettrick and George Smith, came up with the idea that whoever won would be the world flyweight champion, based on the fact that Wilde was the champion of Great Britain while Rosner's managers *claimed* that their man was the champion of America.

On 1 April 1916, Gerald Austin wrote in *Mirror of Life*: 'Who is Johnny Rosner? It seems a curious thing that I have never heard of a potential holder of a world title. In my opinion, Rosner has no more right than the man in the moon to come over here and be boosted as a fitting opponent for Wilde and be a potential wearer of the world flyweight crown.'

The following week, Frank Bradley asked the same question in his editorial, writing that he had received many letters from readers who were also keen to find out who the American was and what credentials he had to make such a claim as being 'champion of all America'.

George Smith sent Bradley a copy of Rosner's record. Unfortunately, Bradley wrongly assumed that Rosner's record was fake – and printed his assumption in his editorial – when he saw the name Jabez White on it. White, who was from Birmingham, had been the English lightweight champion from 1899 to 1906 and was a man Bradley knew well. Bradley asked Jabez if he had ever fought Rosner. Jabez said he had not. However, unbeknown to Bradley, there *was* a very capable bantamweight fighter in America of that name.

What also made Bradley suspicious of Rosner's record was that there were many names on it that were prefixed with the forename 'Young', these being followed by a surname well known in boxing.

Rosner was recorded as having fought 'Young' Ledoux in Montreal. Bradley, wrongly as it turned out, jumped to the conclusion that McKettrick and Smith had sat down and simply written down the word 'Young' and then thought of a well-known fighter (in this case the brilliant Frenchman Charles Ledoux) and used his surname. However, it is quite possible that Rosner *did* fight someone by that name, as Montreal is a French-speaking area. Not only that, but many fighters in America at that time adopted the ring names of their favourite fighters.

Refusing to admit he was wrong, Bradley painstakingly went through his copy of T.S. Andrew's *1916 Boxing Record Book.* In it, Bradley found that Rosner had fought 'Young' Zulu Kid three times in New York, but his fights against Jimmy Curtis, Battling Kilty, Jimmy Paul and Battling Henry were not recorded. This does not mean that they did not take place. As in Britain, record-keeping at that time was patchy to say the least.

Rosner wrote to the editor of *Boxing* on 12 April to put forward his case. 'Although I am unknown in England, this does not mean that I am no good.' Rosner ended the article by admitting that he 'did not hold the American title because the flyweight division did not yet exist in America'.

George Smith wanted Bradley to apologise for what he had written. Bradley steadfastly refused. The following week, Smith wrote to *Mirror of Life*: 'There are hundreds of boxers in America that this gentleman (Bradley) has never heard of who are very good boxers. The record books don't show every fighter in it. Rosner's name was left out purposely. There is no attention paid to the flyweight class in America. A really good one has to fight bantams.'[61]

On 18 April, the *Sporting Chronicle* made the trip to Merseyside to watch Rosner train. Naturally, the subject of his record came up. Smith told the reporter: 'I wish to be insistent on this point. The record I gave Bradley is quite authentic. The Jabez White I mentioned is *not* your old English champion. Why should I be under scrutiny when an English pressman makes a mistake? Some boxing experts over here say they have never heard of the men Rosner has met, yet I have seen old papers in England containing reports of fights that these American boys have engaged in.'

61 *Mirror of Life* 15 April 1916

It was all very unseemly. Bradley and the rest of the boxing writers, quite unfairly, remained sceptical of the visitor. When they watched Rosner training with Tancy Lee in Moreton, near Birkenhead, they reported that they did not think he would 'set the Mersey on fire' and that Rosner was a 'good, second-class man who has no chance against Wilde'.[62]

Charlie Harvey, who had managed 'Peerless' Jim Driscoll and had been an agent for British fighters in America for years, said: 'Young Rosner is quite unknown in America. Can anyone truly believe that he is the champion of America? He may give Wilde a tough fight. He may not. What I object to is that Wilde, who is our accredited champion, is put up against a man who is *not* America's accredited champion and they are said to be fighting for the flyweight championship of the world! If Wilde wins, and I expect him to, he will be no more flyweight champion of the world than I am and trying to kid people that Rosner is the champion of his country is neither sportsmanlike nor honest.'[63]

Nevertheless, Rosner proved to be popular with the locals at his training headquarters at the Farmers Arms Inn at Moreton. He had worked himself into top shape but had to cut his sparring short by five days after clashing heads with one of his sparring partners. Thankfully, Rosner had not been cut, but the clash of heads had left him with a bad swelling on the left side of his temple.

Wilde was experienced enough not to take any notice of the negative comments about the worthiness of his opponent. A list

62 *Mirror of Life* 22 April 1916
63 Ibid

An early photo of Jimmy Wilde at the start of his career

Just one month before he fought for the world title, Tommy Noble gave Jimmy one of his toughest fights (Miles Templeton)

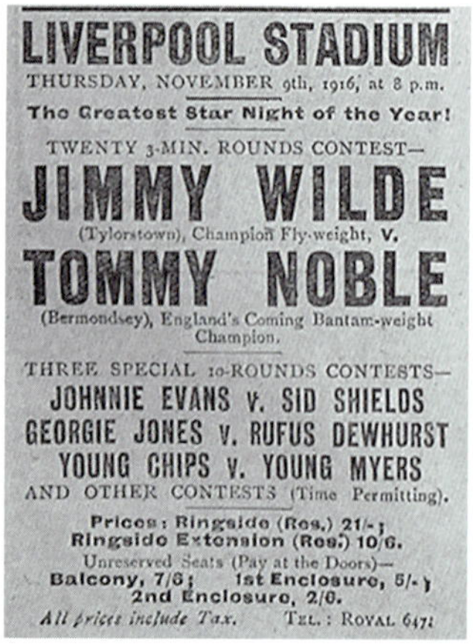

LIVERPOOL STADIUM

THURSDAY, NOVEMBER 9th, 1916, at 8 p.m.

The Greatest Star Night of the Year!

TWENTY 3-MIN. ROUNDS CONTEST—

JIMMY WILDE

(Tylorstown), Champion Fly-weight, v.

TOMMY NOBLE

(Bermondsey), England's Coming Bantam-weight Champion.

THREE SPECIAL 10-ROUNDS CONTESTS—

JOHNNIE EVANS v. SID SHIELDS

GEORGIE JONES v. RUFUS DEWHURST

YOUNG CHIPS v. YOUNG MYERS

AND OTHER CONTESTS (Time Permitting).

Prices: Ringside (Res.) 21/-; Ringside Extension (Res.) 10/6.

Unreserved Seats (Pay at the Doors)—

Balcony, 7/6; 1st Enclosure, 5/-; 2nd Enclosure, 2/6.

All prices include Tax. TEL.: ROYAL 6471

The programme for the Wilde v Zulu Kid fight (Authors collection)

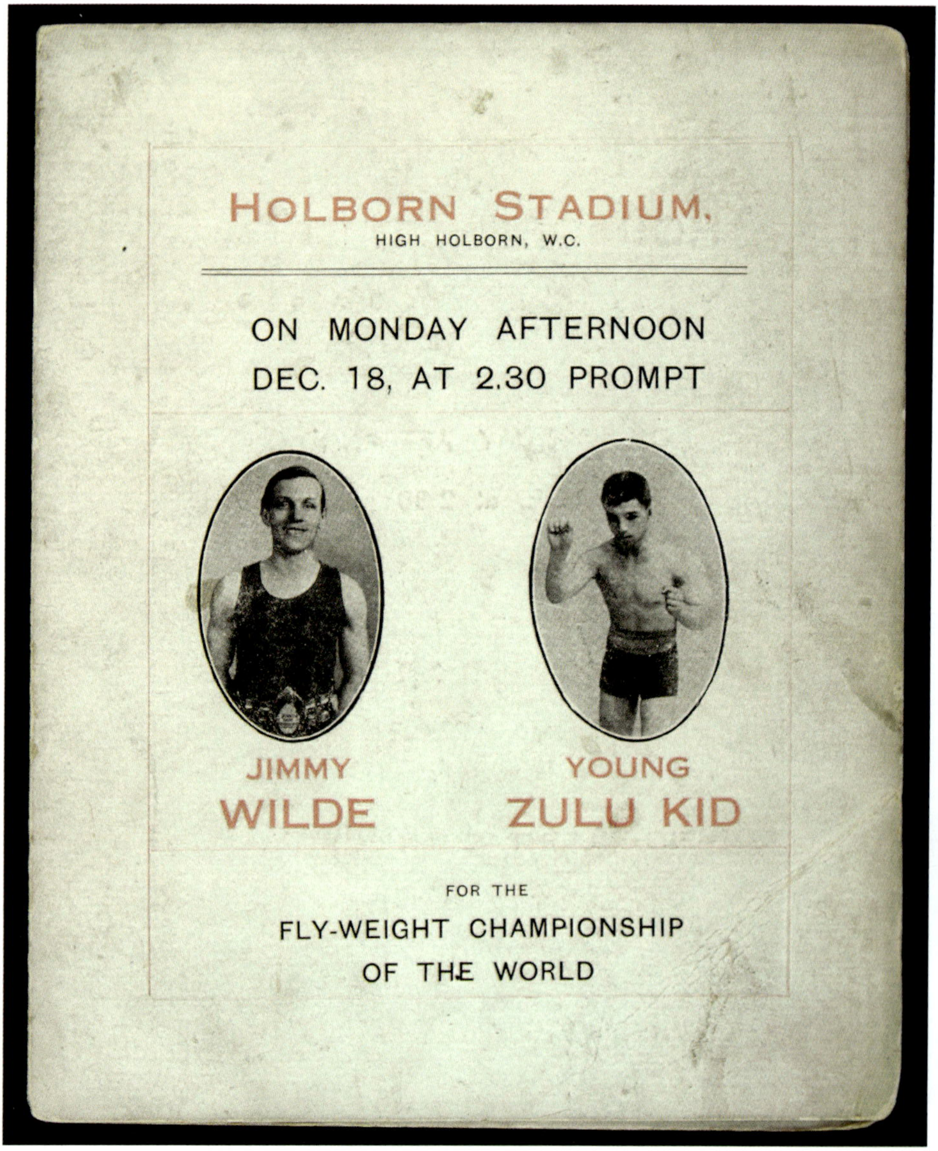

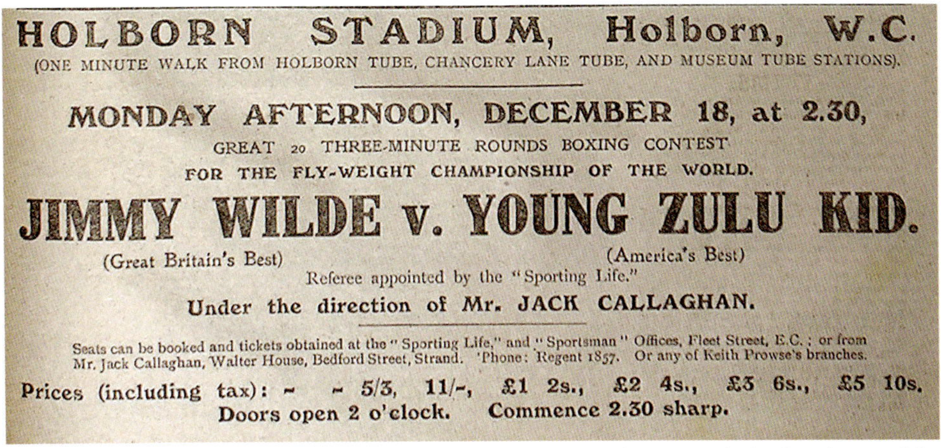

HOLBORN STADIUM, Holborn, W.C.
(ONE MINUTE WALK FROM HOLBORN TUBE, CHANCERY LANE TUBE, AND MUSEUM TUBE STATIONS).

MONDAY AFTERNOON, DECEMBER 18, at 2.30,
GREAT 20 THREE-MINUTE ROUNDS BOXING CONTEST
FOR THE FLY-WEIGHT CHAMPIONSHIP OF THE WORLD.

JIMMY WILDE v. YOUNG ZULU KID.
(Great Britain's Best) (America's Best)
Referee appointed by the "Sporting Life."
Under the direction of Mr. JACK CALLAGHAN.

Seats can be booked and tickets obtained at the "Sporting Life," and "Sportsman" Offices, Fleet Street, E.C.; or from Mr. Jack Callaghan, Walter House, Bedford Street, Strand. 'Phone: Regent 1857. Or any of Keith Prowse's branches.

Prices (including tax): – – 5/3, 11/–, £1 2s., £2 4s., £3 6s., £5 10s.
Doors open 2 o'clock. Commence 2.30 sharp.

The handbill for Wilde's fight with Young Zulu Kid, the first ever fight for the world flyweight title
(Miles Templeton)

Jimmy at home with David (centre), Elizabeth and young Verdun in 1921

A.F. 'Peggy' Bettinson (1862–1926), the man who founded the National Sporting Club and ran British boxing during the first quarter of the 20th century

Note the difference in size between Wilde and Joe Conn in their fight at Stamford Bridge in 1918. Wilde stopped Conn in the 12th round

Wilde is congratulated by HRH the Prince of Wales after outpointing the American Joe Lynch at the NSC on 31 March 1919

Wilde tears after Pal Moore. Olympia, London, 17 July 1919

BOXING, JUNE 16, 1920.
Vol. XXI.—No. 563.

GEORGE CLARK V. VINCE BLACKBURN.

BOXING

PUBLISHED EVERY WEDNESDAY. TWO PENCE.

THE ONLY PAPER IN THE WORLD SOLELY DEVOTED TO BOXING.

Vol. XXI.—No. 563. JUNE 16, 1920. Registered at the General Post Office as a Newspaper and for Canadian Magazine Post.

JIMMY WILDE'S WELCOME HOME TO ENGLAND.

Jimmy and Elizabeth are welcomed home by Jimmy's manager Teddy Lewis on their return from the American tour in June 1920 (Miles Templeton)

Wilde poses with Pancho Villa and referee Patsy Haley moments before the first bell of their fight on 18 June 1923

Jimmy gives some advice to flyweight champ Benny Lynch in 1935

of fights in a record book did not concern him. What Rosner could do in the ring was all that mattered.

On 24 April 1916, Wilde and Rosner met at Pudsey Street. Wilde used the first round to cautiously size up the diminutive American. In the second round, Wilde intentionally threw a few half-hearted punches that fell short to coax Rosner in. Rosner punched back but, tellingly, none of his punches were straight. They were all uncontrolled swings which Wilde easily avoided.

Shortly into the third, Wilde scored with three well-timed rights that staggered Rosner and made him clinch. When the referee broke them apart it became apparent that one of the rights from Wilde had opened a cut on the swelling above Rosner's left eye.

Both boxers were now covered in blood from Rosner's cut and the American fought with an air of desperation about him for the next three rounds, taking everything Wilde could throw at him.

The Liverpool crowd, who no doubt had read the negative press about Rosner, were impressed with his courage and his willingness to keep throwing wide, arching punches in the hope that one might land. By the ninth, however, it was becoming obvious to those at ringside that he would not be able to take much more punishment.

Sensing that the end was near, Rosner threw the kitchen sink at Wilde in the tenth and 11th. To Rosner's frustration, most of his punches missed the target. Both men were milling toe-to-toe in the centre of the ring in the 11th when Rosner's cornerman, Jim Lundie, climbed into the ring to save his man from taking any more.

Rosner, who was totally spent, groggily made his way back to his corner. With the swelling on his head bleeding profusely, both eyes swollen slits and his lips battered purple, Rosner looked a sorry sight as he stood in his corner being attended to by Lundie and Tancy Lee.

The American, who had endured so much unfair negativity in the build-up to the fight (due to Bradley being wrong) had shown tremendous courage and spirit. Thankfully, he did not fall over early as some of the boxing writers had predicted he would. He had taken a tremendous beating without ever troubling Wilde and it was only the compassion of his trainer that prevented him from taking more.

Rosner may not have been the flyweight champion of America that his managers had first claimed him to be on his arrival, but he returned home with his pride intact and his reputation significantly enhanced.

13

A Champion In Demand

THE FIGHT against Johnny Rosner had been an easy workout for Wilde. It had taken so little out of him that five days later he was boxing at the Empire Theatre in Cardiff against Swansea's Benny Thomas.

Wilde received a rapturous ovation as he climbed into the ring. Not many of those watching expected Thomas to last long and even fewer of them expected him to make the fight an interesting spectacle.

The man from Swansea may not have possessed a knockout blow in either hand, but his excellent defence gave Wilde problems in the early rounds. Although he scored at will, Jimmy had few chances to land a big punch that could end the fight. With four rounds left, Thomas attacked more and there were some fast and furious exchanges on the ropes. After 15 entertaining rounds, there was no doubt that Wilde had won a clear decision.

The Wilde household was a happy one in the spring of 1916. Jimmy and Elizabeth had a two-month-old boy to keep them busy, Jimmy had his cherished Lonsdale belt on display on the fireplace and, to top it all off, he was building up a healthy nest egg thanks to his earnings from fights and personal appearances.

All Wilde wanted now was a return match with Tancy Lee. He desperately wanted to avenge the only loss he had ever suffered and Lee, providing he could make 8st without weakening himself, was the only real test out there for him.

The boxing writers were of the same opinion. Tancy strengthened his claim even further when he stopped Joe Symonds in the 17th round at Plymouth on 5 May. The fight, which was at bantamweight, had been going Symonds's way until Tancy caught him with a smashing right cross that took everything out of him.

Tancy's win over Symonds had come at the right time for Wilde. 'Peggy' Bettinson was keen to see a rematch and, when Lee assured Bettinson that he could comfortably make 8st given enough time, the fight (for £500 a side, equal to around £36,000 a side in 2024) was scheduled for 26 June at the National Sporting Club.

In the meantime, Teddy Lewis was busy batting away offers from opponents Wilde had already beaten. The wily veteran, Dido Gains, offered to fight Wilde for £100 a side over 20 two-minute rounds. Lewis promptly told the Gains camp that Wilde was now only taking part in fights with three-minute rounds and that if they agreed to this – and Gains's backers were prepared to pay £500 a side – then they would have their fight. Lewis went on to tell them that, as champion, it was preposterous to expect Wilde to fight for £100 a side, a purse that he had been fighting for three years prior to winning the title.

Jimmy was more than happy to fight anybody, but the Gains offer had been hopeful to say the least, especially with Wilde's British title at stake. Lewis knew Wilde's worth as the champion. If rival managers wanted to challenge him for his belt, then they would have to put up the right money.

Non-title fights against second-rate opposition were a different matter. In May of 1916, London promoter Harry Williams contacted Teddy Lewis with a proposition. Would Wilde be willing to have two fights in one afternoon in front of the troops at Woolwich? Lewis, knowing that Wilde would never say no to helping out the servicemen, agreed at once.

On 13 May at the Theatre Royal in Woolwich, Wilde fought Darkie Saunders, who he had beaten twice before in 1913, and Young Magnus from Wapping.

It turned out to be an afternoon of great entertainment for the soldiers of the Royal Artillery, who were based nearby. Saunders, who was very much at the veteran stage of his career, had no chance and was pulled out by the referee in the third round. Poor Young Magnus was knocked clean out by a perfectly timed right in the second.

Wilde loved chatting to the soldiers and signing autographs at such events. He got a deep feeling of satisfaction from knowing he could provide a couple of hours of entertainment to take the soldiers' minds off the war.

Wilde had been enthused by his recent appearance at Woolwich. The idea of joining up had been gnawing away at him ever since he had been rejected in Birmingham; meeting the soldiers at Woolwich had further fuelled the feeling that he wanted to do his duty.

When he returned home, Wilde went down to the recruitment office in Cardiff. After his medical, and a long wait, a member of the medical board called Wilde back into the office. This time, Wilde had been rejected for military service due to being underweight.[64]

Wilde was disappointed and confused. 'It is almost impossible for me to believe that it actually happened,' he would later recall. 'Even with the Lonsdale belt as my proud possession, I was passed unfit for active service.'[65]

For Wilde, it was frustrating. Even so, he had to try to put it to the back of his mind and be content, for now, with helping the war effort by raising money by appearing in exhibitions.

As opposed to nowadays, when Wilde would have gone away to a state-of-the-art training camp for three months before fights, he warmed up for his bout with Tancy Lee by fighting an incredibly tough and durable bantamweight who, just one month before, had gone the distance with the British bantamweight champion.

Tommy Harrison, from Hanley, Stoke-on-Trent, had his first fight in 1909 at the age of 17. A classical upright boxer with a brilliant jab, Harrison learnt his trade fighting in Burslem and Newcastle-under-Lyme.

Harrison had beaten some good men as he came through the ranks, including Johnny Best, Dido Gains, Alf Mansfield

---

64 At around the same time, Owen Moran, who had fought for the world lightweight title in 1911, was rejected for having chipped bones in his hands.

65 Jimmy Wilde *Fighting Was My Business* p.105

and Louis Ruddick. Although he had been outpointed by Bill Ladbury and Joe Symonds, as well as being stopped in eight by Percy Jones, Harrison was a top calibre fighter who had only lost to the very best. In May 1914, Harrison lost a ten-round decision to Tancy Lee in a final eliminator for the vacant flyweight title.

After going into his fight with Tancy Lee severely weight-drained, Harrison wisely decided to stay at bantamweight from then on. Over the next two years, he built up a 13-1-3 record and earned a shot at the British bantamweight title held by Leeds's Joe Fox. In a close fight that could have gone either way, it was Fox who had his hand raised after 20 rounds.

The ornate setting that was the Oxford Music Hall in Oxford Street, London, was the venue for Wilde's fight with Harrison on 29 May 1916. Harrison was first to climb into the ring and quietly sat in his corner waiting. As Wilde climbed through the ropes, the orchestra struck up 'See The Conquering Hero Comes'. *Boxing* wondered why the orchestra had not afforded the Hanley boxer the same welcome on his way to the ring.

Harrison, whose overall record was 34-11-1, spent the first half of the opening round trying to catch Wilde with a significant punch. Wilde avoided every one of them and scored with his jab. A hard right to Wilde's body made him wince and Harrison drove him to the ropes, but Harrison could not make the shot count as Wilde slipped and dodged his way out of danger.

Harrison was intent on attacking Wilde hard, but what he gave out he got back with twice as much force. By the end of the second round, Harrison's nose had started to swell and his left eye was closing. 'Wilde was merciless,' wrote *Boxing*. 'Dancing and dodging round his victim, Wilde shot home left after left – stinging stabs all of them – rarely, if ever, missing.'

In the third, Wilde lifted Harrison's head back with a perfectly timed uppercut. Harrison retaliated with a right to the stomach but was off balance and fell into a clinch. Wilde threw the heavier man to the boards. Harrison got up but was met by a heavy left to the body that put him down for a short count.

At the start of the fourth, Tommy bullied Wilde to the ropes, where both men whaled away at each other for a full minute. When Harrison stood off, Wilde dropped him again in the centre of the ring with a right to the jaw. Rising after a count of four, Harrison got his own back by landing another hard right to Wilde's body.

Both men swung at each other for all they were worth in the fifth. A smashing right to Harrison's jaw dropped him again. This time, Harrison rose at eight.

Harrison, in an attempt to slow Wilde down, thudded home a right to his body early in the sixth. The blow made Wilde hold on. Wilde 'ducked under Harrison's left arm and gave us all a lesson in the art of avoiding. For fully 40 seconds, he dodged without attempting to hit back and defied Harrison to touch him, until he went back to the old jabbing game.' [66]

Wilde seemed intent on ending the fight in the seventh. Both Harrison's eyes were now nearly closed and his nose and lips were badly damaged. A terrific right from Wilde sent two of Harrison's

66 *Boxing* 31 May 1916

teeth flying out of his mouth. Another right put Tommy down for a seven count just before the bell.

Harrison dashed over to Wilde at the start of the eighth, throwing lefts and rights. It was one last desperate effort from a courageous man. When Harrison realised that most of his punches had missed and was then met with an onslaught of lefts and rights to the face, he took a step back and waved his glove in surrender.[67]

Now all attention turned to Tancy Lee. *Boxing* wrote that Lee had made a big mistake in not going to see Wilde fight Harrison. In truth, with Wilde in such scintillating form, it was probably a good thing for Tancy that he had decided not to. The big question was whether Tancy was going to crowd Wilde, as he had done in their first fight, or was he going to stand off and box from distance. Either way, *Boxing* was going with the man who had the heavier punch, which was Wilde.

Tancy prepared for the fight at the Black Bull Inn at Whetstone, where he would rise early every morning and go for a ten-mile walk. Tancy would then have breakfast and rest until early afternoon, when he would spar in the gym and do his skipping and groundwork.

Meanwhile, in Tylorstown, Wilde started his day with a round of golf before breakfast. 'His complexion has undergone a marked change,' reported *The Sportsman*. 'He has spent so much time in the open air that he is more like a gypsy than the pallid

67 Harrison served in France and was gassed in 1917. He made a full recovery and returned to the ring two years later. He won the British bantamweight title from Jim Higgins in 1922 but lost it to Bugler Harry Lake the following year. Harrison died of meningitis on 17 May 1931, aged 38. He was married with three daughters.

little fellow that we have so often seen.'[68]

On the night of 26 June 1916, a hush descended around the National Sporting Club as the two boxers waited for the bell. The speculation in regards to how Tancy was going to approach the fight was answered straight away. He was going to fight Wilde exactly the same way he had done the first time, by bustling him to the ropes and fighting in close.

Tancy was hoping that his superior natural strength would take its toll on Wilde as it had before. Only this time, Wilde was fully fit. In their first fight, when Wilde had been trapped on the ropes, he had not had the strength to escape. This time, he *did* have the strength. He was able to duck, weave and slide away back to the centre of the ring.

A loud gasp emanated throughout the hall in the second when Lee connected flush with a left on Wilde's jaw. Wilde felt it but was not shaken. He now knew he could take Tancy's best punch and not be hurt by it. He also knew Tancy could not outbox him. The fight was there for him, but he knew it would take time to break the resolve of the teak-tough Scot.

The third round was a torrid one for both of them. For nearly the entire round, Wilde and Tancy punched each other non-stop to head and body along the ropes.

Lee rushed Wilde to the ropes at the start of the fourth, but Wilde managed to slip away and shade the round with his left jabs. In the fifth, Tancy again pinned Wilde to the ropes. This was his only real chance to land any telling blows. The tactic

68 *The Sportsman* 21 June 1916

nearly backfired for Lee, however. A left uppercut followed by a left and a right shook him to his boots just as the bell sounded.

Tancy leant all his weight on Wilde during the sixth and seventh, but Wilde got the better of the exchanges in close. The close-quarter action continued in the eighth round, from which Wilde emerged with a slight cut over his left eye.

Worried by the cut, Wilde had a shaky start to the ninth when Tancy landed several hurtful body blows, but Wilde gathered himself and hurt Lee with a left hook to the chin and a left-right to the body. Tancy looked drained and weary as he went back to his corner.

At the start of the tenth, Tancy looked all of his 34 years. A left-right combination to Tancy's body brought his hands down. Wilde, seeing Tancy's unprotected jaw, connected with a right that made him totter backwards. Wilde went after him with a hail of lefts and rights which forced Tancy down on one knee for a count of nine. Another fusillade of punches made Tancy touch down on one knee for a second time. Up at eight, Wilde kept on punching until Tancy went down on one knee again. Tancy rose again at eight, but Wilde was on him like a flash. A left hook followed by a smashing straight right knocked Tancy clean off his feet as the bell went. His cornermen jumped through the ropes and lifted him back to his corner where they drenched him in water in an effort to revive him.

Tancy was a beaten man as the bell clanged for round 11. Four body punches from Wilde with alternate hands made Tancy give ground. A right to Tancy's ribs made him sink to one knee. The crowd were now shouting for the referee to stop it, but somehow Tancy got up at six. But, before he knew it, Wilde had hit him with a right to the chin and a left to the side of the head, knocking the Leith man off his feet. Tancy was out as referee Douglas waved Wilde away.[69]

Teddy Lewis was now having difficulty finding fighters who were willing to boil themselves down to 8st to fight Wilde, whose main wish now was to defend his Lonsdale belt once more at the National Sporting Club so that the belt would be his to keep.

Boxing wanted to see Wilde challenge the British bantamweight champion Joe Fox. It would have been a very good fight had it been made. Wilde would definitely have fancied his chances, even though he would have been conceding around 22lb to the champion.

The only other candidate at that time was Bloomsbury's Johnny Hughes. He was more than willing to fight Wilde when terms were put to him, even if it meant having to sweat off 4lb, and the fight was scheduled for 31 July. However, to Wilde's dismay, the fight would be at Kensal Rise Athletic Ground and not the National Sporting Club.

In 1911, Hughes was a top flyweight who fully expected to be challenging Sid Smith for the inaugural British title. When the National Sporting Club nominated Joe Wilson to fight Smith instead, Hughes called the hierarchy at the NSC 'a bunch of

69 After his loss to Wilde, Lee won the Scottish bantamweight title and then won the British featherweight title by beating Charlie Hardcastle in 1917. He retired in 1921 and became an amateur coach at Leith Victoria ABC. Lee died in 1941 after being hit by a bus in Edinburgh. He was 59.

autocrats'. The committee promptly banned him from fighting there ever again.

In 1912, a disillusioned Hughes set sail for America, where he cemented his claim to be one of Britain's best little men by fighting a six-round 'no decision' bout with Kid Williams in Philadelphia. Williams, who was a class operator, would go on to win the world bantamweight championship two years later by beating Johnny Coulon in Los Angeles.

By the time he fought Wilde, Hughes was 34 and in the twilight of a long and hard career. During the 18 years he had been fighting, Hughes had met everybody in and around his weight, from Bill Beynon, Charles Ledoux and Bill Ladbury to Alf Mansfield, Sid Shields, Sam Keller, Tancy Lee and Joe Symonds.

They say that the last thing a fighter loses is his punch and that seemed to be the case for Hughes. In the week leading up to the Wilde fight, the papers reported that he had burst six punchballs in training. The statement had a certain amount of irony to it. After all, a 'puncher's chance' was the only *real* chance that any of the boxing writers were giving him.

The open air show at Kensal Rise got off to an inauspicious start. During the introductions, the master of ceremonies invited Alf Mansfield, who was sitting at ringside, to climb into the ring to take a bow. As Mansfield did so, the MC welcomed him into the ring by announcing him as 'the only man in Great Britain who can give Wilde a fight'. It was a gross insult to Hughes, who was warming up in his corner. *Boxing* was aghast at the slight. 'Can you wonder what Hughes must have felt?' they asked. 'Wasn't Hughes going to essay that very task himself?'

A professional of Hughes's standing deserved better. If he was angry at the slight, he did not show it once the bell rang. He came out in a crouch with his arms crossed over his face and carefully stalked Wilde around the ring, trying to get in range so he could land his jab.

With Hughes in a defensive shell, Wilde scored at will with lefts and rights. Despite Hughes's best efforts to cover up, most of Wilde's punches were piercing his guard and, by the end of the second round, his face was beginning to redden.

In the third, Hughes bullied Wilde to the ropes, where he had marginally more success. In close, Hughes fired punches at Wilde's body and drew his ire by repeatedly hitting him around the kidneys.

By the fifth, Hughes had been reduced to throwing wild swings and these were missing. Wilde countered with lefts and rights and, by the end of the round, Hughes's left eye was starting to swell shut.

'Time and again Johnny hurled himself at Wilde but rarely managed to get anything home. Try as he might, Hughes just could not corner the little wonder, whose dodging and ducking were simply amazing.'[70]

Every time Hughes attempted to punch, he was made to miss and then punished with left-right-left-right combinations.

As Hughes came out for the tenth, the large crowd had an inkling he would not be able to last much longer. Hughes rushed

70 *Boxing* 2 August 1916

at Wilde but missed and went into the ropes. As he half-turned to face Wilde, he was met with a right uppercut and a left hook. Hughes dropped his arms. Wilde measured him with his left and then delivered the knockout blow, a devastating right to Hughes's jaw that sent the brave Londoner face-first to the canvas. As the referee completed the count, Hughes got to his feet, only for his legs to collapse under him. His cornermen rushed into the ring to carry him back to his stool.

14

The Zulu Kid

BY THE summer of 1916, the war had been raging for far longer than people had ever expected and the number of young men who were willing to enlist had fallen drastically due to the high rate of casualties. Boxing, which was as popular at this time as it had ever been, was being used as a key tool to recruit young men into the army. Boxing instilled discipline, physical fitness and self-control. Exactly the attributes needed to be a good, efficient soldier.

But it was not only taking part in boxing that had flourished. Watching boxing as a pastime had always been popular, but now shows – especially military tournaments – were attracting huge crowds. Boxing was proving to be a welcome distraction from the horrors people were reading about every morning in their newspapers. The boxers themselves, especially national champions, had not been lionised and held in such high regard since the days of the old London Prize Ring.

The announcement that Jimmy Wilde was to appear at a military boxing tournament was always a guarantee to the organisers of the event that they would have a capacity crowd.

This is how Wilde spent the summer of 1916. He toured all around Britain taking on soldiers in exhibition bouts alongside Bombadier Billy Wells, the British heavyweight champion, Johnny Basham, the British welterweight champion, Bandsman Jack Blake, the British middleweight champion, and former British middleweight champion Pat O'Keefe.

A measure of the boxers' popularity was the crowd of more than 4,000 at Southampton Football Club to watch this group of elite fighters show off their skills in good-natured exhibitions. Nearly 2,000 of those who attended were wounded soldiers. A similar number turned out at The Hawthorns, the home of West Bromwich Albion, where the funds raised went to the British Sportsmen's Motor Ambulance Fund.

Despite Wilde's popularity, there were people who were at a loss as to why he had not joined up, even though the reasons had been made public in regional and national newspapers. On more than one occasion, Wilde was heckled in the street by people who thought he should be in uniform. Wilde had shown time and again in the ring that he could physically outlast men who were a stone heavier than himself, yet he had still been passed unfit for service.

It was a situation that weighed heavily on Wilde's mind even though, outwardly, he did not show it. He felt a constant desire to do something to help. 'Many people thought that I was pulling my weight by fighting, but it did not entirely satisfy me,' he would later write. 'There were grumblers. Accusations of cowardice. Threats of being sent a white feather.'[71]

---

71 Jimmy Wilde *Fighting Was My Business* p.123

Some believed Wilde was being given preferential treatment because of his fame as a boxer. There is no doubt that he was making a lot of money for both himself and boxing promoters up and down the land. If he was enlisted, some reasoned, then that considerable income for both parties would stop.

There is no doubt that the substantial amounts Wilde was earning from boxing caused feelings of resentment among some in the Welsh valleys. Many were having to care for a loved one who had been sent home seriously injured. Many were living on the breadline. Reading about a boxer, albeit a great one, earning £500 in one evening did not sit well with them, no matter how much he had raised through attending charity events.

Wilde, however, had made it clear on numerous occasions that he *wanted* to join up. He had turned down several lucrative offers to go to America so that he would be readily available.

The boxing press was firmly behind him. The only thing boxing writers were concerned about was who Jimmy was going to fight next. As far as they were concerned, if the army medical board had declared him unfit, then that was the end of the matter.

Towards the end of September, Teddy Lewis and Jack Callaghan of the Liverpool Sporting Syndicate met to discuss potential opponents for Wilde. Callaghan, who had been instrumental in bringing over Rosner, thought that another American would be a good idea, mainly because he wanted to promote a fight that could be advertised as being for the 'world flyweight championship'. Jimmy Pappas, a Greek-born bantamweight who lived in Atlanta, Georgia, was the first to be considered but, after much thought, he was deemed not to have strong enough credentials. Callaghan and Lewis did not want a repeat of the dodgy record saga that they had endured with Rosner, even though it was a British-based writer who had started that dispute.

Eventually, after many telegraphed messages across the Atlantic, Lewis and Callaghan settled on a fighter who had been given the moniker 'the Fighting Newsboy' by the American press and fought under the name Young Zulu Kid.

Young Zulu Kid was born Giuseppe De Melfi in Potenza, Italy, on 22 April 1897. When Giuseppe was still an infant, his family emigrated to New York City in search of work and a new life. They settled in the Italian section of Brooklyn, where young Giuseppe spent his time street fighting with other boys from rival neighbourhoods.

Standing 4ft 11in tall and weighing around 7st 10lb, Young Zulu Kid's earliest recorded fights were from around 1912 onwards. A rugged, light-punching, come-forward fighter, most of his fights had taken place in Brooklyn's athletic clubs against local fighters in 'no decision' bouts.[72]

Like Wilde, Young Zulu Kid had to concede weight in the majority of his fights. There simply weren't enough flyweights in America at that time, so he found himself having to face bantamweights.

72 The no decision era ran from 1900–1920 during which time professional boxing was illegal in many US states, including New York. From 1911-1920 the Frawley Law permitted boxing only in private clubs. Fights that went the distance had neither a winner nor a loser. To win, a fighter had to score a KO. No decision bouts, however, gave birth to the term 'Newspaper decision.' Local reporters, who had watched the fights from ringside, gave their opinion on who they thought had won and printed their 'unofficial' results in the paper the following day.

Even so, for such a tiny man, the Kid was immensely strong. He looked more like a weightlifter than a boxer, with thick forearms and tightly bunched biceps. His face, however, could not hide the fact that he earned his living by fighting. His eyebrows were thick set with scar tissue, his nose looked like it had taken many blows and his left ear was totally disfigured.

According to *BoxRec*, Young Zulu Kid had taken part in 65 'no decision' bouts by the time he fought Wilde and he had never been stopped, even though he had fought in excellent company. He had gone the distance with Johnny Ertle, Johnny Rosner (twice), future world bantamweight champion Pete Herman (twice) and Pal Moore (three times).

Throughout the autumn of 1916, Lewis and Callaghan discussed terms with the Kid's manager, Jocy Sarno. The fight was set for 18 December. They were more than happy to sail to England, even though Callaghan did not have a venue for the fight. With the contest being for the inaugural world flyweight title, Callaghan insisted the fight be held in London. Ideally, Callaghan wanted it to be at the Royal Albert Hall, but he claimed the venue wanted too much money to stage it, forcing him to look for an alternative.

Callaghan, who was an intrepid businessman if ever there was one, kept looking. Quite fortuitously, he stumbled upon an abandoned building in Holborn that had once been the Central Hall. Callaghan was so confident that he could get the building ready in time that he told *Boxing* in early October that it would be ready within two months. Not many believed him.

In fighting for a world title, Wilde found himself in a curious position. To him, it felt like just another fight. At any other weight, fighting for a world title was the pinnacle of a boxer's career. The flyweight division, however, had only been in existence for seven years. During that time, it had been dominated by British boxers. To all intents and purposes, it was a British division. There were few men fighting at 8st in continental Europe or in America who were of any great standard. At that time, winning a Lonsdale belt was the most prestigious prize for a British flyweight.

Most boxing insiders were of the opinion that a bout between Wilde and another Englishman at the National Sporting Club would have meant more than a fight against a relatively unknown American. However, by staging a fight between a British and an American fighter, Callaghan, whether he realised it or not, was setting a precedent that was only going to benefit boxing's newest weight class in the long term. Within 20 years, the flyweight division would evolve from a weight class dominated by British fighters into a truly international one.

In the meantime, Wilde was preparing to meet Leeds bantamweight Louis Ruddick. The Yorkshireman had been wanting to fight Wilde for some time and had repeatedly made his intentions known in the sporting papers. However, despite his best efforts, he found it impossible to get down to the 8st 4lb limit that both parties had agreed on. Ruddick had no option but to pull out of the fight.

A new opponent had to be found quickly. Tommy Noble, the 19-year-old from Bermondsey who Wilde had beaten ten months earlier, stepped in. Since he had lost to Wilde, Noble had fought an astonishing 25 times (16-7-2) against some of the country's best bantamweights and featherweights.

Prior to the fight, there were rumours that Noble was having trouble getting down to 8st 4lb. There was a fair bit of anxiety in the air when he stepped on to the scales in Liverpool. To everyone's relief, Noble was 1oz inside the agreed limit.

Noble came out fast in the opening two rounds, swinging lefts and rights. Wilde avoided most of them by swaying back and neatly countered with well-timed lefts. In the third, Wilde drove Noble to the ropes. A left followed by a thunderous right knocked Noble to the canvas. Noble rose quickly but he looked groggy as he sat on his stool.

Noble had recovered well during the one-minute interval, which was a testament to his fitness and conditioning. While Wilde was a little too anxious and was made to miss, Noble confidently countered him with rights. His efforts drew applause as he went back to his corner.

Both men were boxing well and taking it in turns to score. By the end of the sixth, there was little between them, but Wilde got the upper hand when he floored Noble with a straight right midway through the seventh. Noble got up and wisely went on the defensive until the bell.

After a quiet eighth, the fight came alive in the ninth. Wilde scored with a powerful right to the body that forced Noble to go down on one knee for a five count. Knowing that Noble was hurt, Wilde steamed into the Londoner, but Noble hung on and then began to score with his left and the odd right cross.

Uncharacteristically, Wilde was still looking for that one big knockout blow in the tenth. Round 11 saw Wilde throw himself off his feet when a right sailed over Noble's head.

In the 12th, Wilde found himself in the most precarious situation of his career so far. Noble dropped Wilde with a pulverising right to the jaw. Wilde got up at five but was groggy. Noble rushed in and sent over another right. Wilde went down again. By now the Pudsey Street crowd were in a state of pandemonium. Wilde got to his feet at eight but his body was limp as he leaned against the ropes for support. Those in the cheap seats must have been convinced Wilde was beaten, but those closer to the ring noticed that, when the two resumed fighting, the thought of victory had overcome Noble. He could hardly believe what he had just done. One more solid blow would have put Wilde down and out. Instead, Noble was over-eager and flailed away. Wilde, thinking only of survival, covered up and waited for what seemed like forever for the bell to ring.

Driscoll worked feverishly on Wilde during the interval, vigorously massaging the back of Wilde's neck. Teddy Lewis shouted instructions into his ear and threw a sponge of cold water in his face. One minute had never gone so quickly.

Wilde was still badly dazed. His legs were not responding to what his brain was telling them. Knowing that his legs would betray him if he got on his bicycle, Wilde stood in front of Noble in the 13th and tried his best to slip the punches that were being thrown his way.

In the 14th round, Noble held and wrestled Wilde at every opportunity, which drew a warning from the referee. Noble was hoping that leaning on Wilde would tire him even more, but it afforded Wilde time to recover.

Coming out for the 15th, Noble was exhausted. Wilde's head had cleared. He tore after Noble like a terrier. A straight right put Noble down. He got up on shaky legs. Wilde dropped him three more times in quick succession. On rising after the last of these knockdowns, the referee had seen enough and waved off the fight.

From somewhere deep within himself, Wilde had dredged up an inner strength that saw him over the line. Teddy Lewis was mightily relieved and philosophical. 'We are glad this has happened. Nothing could be better. It will be a valuable lesson to us.'[73]

Tommy Noble had given Wilde a tremendous fight – and a tremendous fright – in Liverpool. Teddy Lewis was correct in his assessment. Wilde had been over-confident. Coming so perilously close to defeat would only help Wilde to refocus and remember to take nothing for granted. On the other hand, Wilde had proved that there was nothing wrong with his powers of recovery. Nevertheless, he did not want too many fights like the one Tommy Noble had given him.

Young Zulu Kid and his manager, Joey Sarno, arrived at Southampton in November amid little fanfare.

---

73 *Boxing* 15 November 1916

At his training headquarters in Brighton, the Kid sparred with Alf Mansfield and did his roadwork along the bracing seafront. One visiting reporter described him as 'a pocket Hercules who has the arms of a middleweight'.[74]

Sarno was friendly and approachable to the press, but was keen to avoid another Rosner situation. 'We do not claim anything or come here with a manufactured record,' he told *Mirror of Life*. 'We have heard and read all about Wilde. All we can say is that we will do the best we can and that – win, lose or draw – we will give the public a run for their money. I believe every true sportsman appreciates a boy's best efforts and that is what we are going to give.'[75]

Meanwhile, Wilde trained at home with Benny Williams, Jim Driscoll and sparring partners Dai 'Chips' Davies, Billy Fry, Gomer Evans and George Jones. *Boxing* expected Wilde to win with plenty to spare. It agreed with most of the sportswriters who had seen the Kid in training. If the American was to have any chance of winning then he must get inside and fight in close; if he chose to fight at long range, then he would be comprehensively outboxed and stopped.

The ever-cautious Teddy Lewis did not give an answer when pressed on Wilde's chances; instead, he diplomatically told the boxing scribes that Wilde had 'finished his preparations in great shape and, providing nothing unforeseen happens in the meantime, he will enter the ring physically perfect'.

Callaghan, who had been under tremendous strain for nigh-on three months, had been true to his word. The Holborn arena

74 *The Sportsman* 7 December 1916
75 *Mirror of Life* 25 November 1916

was finished in time for the fight. Not only that, Callaghan had spared no expense during the refurbishment in what *Boxing* described as 'one of the most wonderful feats British workmen have ever achieved'.[76]

On the afternoon of Monday, 18 December 1916, the Holborn stadium was filled to its 5,000-seat capacity as Wilde and the Kid stepped through the ropes. When the referee, J.T. Hulls, called them to the centre of the ring for their final instructions, the three-and-a-half-inch height advantage Wilde had over the Kid became starkly apparent. For the American to have any chance, he would have to attack Wilde's body, despite him being known as a light puncher. The crowd was so confident that Wilde would win that the betting was on how many rounds the Kid would last rather than who would win the fight. It turned out that many punters lost their money because they backed Wilde to win within the first three rounds.

At 4.30pm, the first bell sounded. Both men led off with their lefts, but both men blocked or parried each other's punches in a quiet opener.

In the second round, the Italian-American introduced his crouch-and-spring movement. The Kid would bend his knees until he looked as if he was in a sitting position without a chair and would then leap forwards, throwing lefts and rights. At first, this took Wilde by surprise but, by the time the Kid had repeated the move four or five times, Wilde did not wait for him to spring and simply jabbed the top of his head.

76 *Boxing* 27 December 1916

The round had been a relatively uneventful one until Wilde landed a left uppercut, the force of which lifted the Kid's head. Wilde, sensing his opponent was hurt, immediately followed up with a right cross which made the Kid stagger backwards. Wilde stepped towards him and landed three more vicious rights to the jaw that sent the Kid tumbling to the canvas. The Kid was out to the world. Before the referee could start his count, the bell clanged to save the American. His cornermen rushed into the ring and unceremoniously lifted the Kid off the floor and carried him back to his corner.

Somehow, the one-minute interval between rounds was enough for him to come back round. Wilde undoubtedly thought that he could end it early, but the Kid shuffled forward with a cross-arm defence and, by the end of the round, he was even starting to score with his own shots to Wilde's body.

In the fourth round, the Kid nearly got tagged with what would have been a fight-ending right after he had missed with a left of his own, but he showed tremendous poise by retreating into his defensive shell. Wilde made sure the round was his when he forced the Kid to the ropes and landed a left-right-left-right-left-right combination on the bell.

The Kid was still strong in the fifth and took most of Wilde's punches on his crossed arms. Wilde, unlike in his fight with Noble, seemed to have ice in his veins and carefully measured his punches. Just to remind Wilde that he was still in the fight, the Kid landed a few thudding shots that were close to Wilde's kidneys.

Wilde was unintentionally hit low at the start of the sixth, but the blow did not unduly bother him. Wilde then drove the Kid backwards with a two-fisted barrage to head and body. The Kid was looking weary as he was pummelled on the ropes and many observers thought he was about to go down, but he found two left hooks and a right to momentarily shake Wilde seconds before the end of the round.

The Kid had his best round of the fight in the seventh. Although he missed a great deal, a sharp left hook got Wilde's attention and Jimmy had to use all of his slipping and ducking skills to avoid the Kid's incessant blows.

A good left hook from Wilde shook the Kid early in the eighth. The Kid replied with a fast right and left which drew Wilde into a fast and furious rally. Both men punched each other around the ring, but it was the Kid who had to give ground and find solace by covering and clinching on the ropes.

The man from Brooklyn took the fight to Wilde in the ninth, which bought the crowd to its feet. A left hook in close visibly shook Wilde and he was compelled to fight back with two-handed rallies.

Coming out for the tenth, Wilde had clearly made up his mind to properly stamp his authority on the contest. A left hook shook the American to his toes at the start of the round. The Kid momentarily fought back, but he was met with stinging left jabs and thumping right crosses that made him go on the defensive.

As the bell sounded for round 11, the Kid still looked sprightly as he came out of his corner and met Wilde in the centre of the ring with both arms crossed over his face. Wilde scored with a jab and a right. A left hook to the side of the head drove the Kid backwards into his own corner. Wilde pounced. A dozen lefts and rights rained down on the Kid. Just as he collapsed to the canvas, his corner threw in the towel. 'The Zulu Kid was out to the world after one of the most wonderful displays of gameness and stamina on record.'[77]

77 *Boxing* 27 December 1916

15
Sandhurst And A Bag Of Diamonds

A COUPLE of days after Christmas 1916, Wilde once again went to the recruitment office in Cardiff. To his great relief, and at the third time of asking, he passed the medical. This time, somewhat oddly, no mention was made of his weak leg or of him being underweight, even though he was in the same physical condition he had been during the two previous examinations. The only change for Wilde had been that, since his second failed attempt, he had become a world champion.

By the time he was accepted into the army, the war had been raging for two years and four months. Wilde now hoped that the snide remarks from some sections of the public would stop.

Boxing rebuked those who had criticised Wilde. 'Those gentlemen who wield facile pens but are not in khaki themselves will have to look for another peg on which to hang their abuse. They now ought to confess that the army's medical authorities, who rejected him twice, knew more about the physical requirements than they did themselves.'[78]

---

78 *Boxing* 3 January 1917

Initially, Wilde expected to be sent to northern France on garrison duty but, in early January, he was informed that he was going to be a physical training instructor at Aldershot.

While undergoing training there, Wilde would be with his old pals Bombardier Billy Wells, Johnny Basham, Dick Smith, Jim Driscoll and Pat O'Keefe. Under the watchful eye of Capt. Bruce Logan, this group of elite boxers became widely known as 'the Famous Six'. They had spent the previous summer touring Britain fighting in exhibitions which had proved to be immensely popular and many more were planned for 1917.

Even though joining up had silenced those who had abused him verbally and in print for not being enlisted sooner, Wilde was worried. As an elite sportsman, it was highly unlikely that he would be sent to the Western Front. Even so, the thought he might be sent to France or Belgium, where he could be shot or blown to smithereens in a muddy field, quite naturally filled him with dread. Like everyone else over the past two-and-a-half years, Wilde had read the daily newspaper reports of the tens of thousands of soldiers who had been maimed and killed on foreign soil. It was horrific and, worse still, there seemed to be no end in sight to the carnage.

Shortly before he was due to report to Aldershot in late January, Wilde became so anxious that he wrote to the Rhondda Recruitment Tribunal asking for an exemption. Wilde told the tribunal that he had worked underground for ten years as a miner, which was a reserved occupation, and that he had twice been medically rejected for the army. In his opinion, he informed them, he would be far more use to the country working underground in Tylorstown.

The chairman of the tribunal disagreed. In his opinion, Wilde, due to his great sporting prowess, would be of more use getting soldiers into peak physical condition. The chairman, in summing up, told Wilde that 'in view of the great needs of the country, I do not see much hope that your application will be successful'.[79]

Wilde's application was, indeed, unsuccessful. A member of the army top brass immediately reassured Wilde by post, telling him that being a physical training instructor was a plum job and that, as a world champion boxer and popular public figure, he would not be sent abroad to fight. Furthermore, after basic training at Aldershot, Wilde would be posted to the Royal Military Academy at Sandhurst later in the year, where he would have a good job training officers. First-class accommodation for Elizabeth and the children was being provided and he would also be granted extra leave as and when required.

Wilde, like most newly recruited soldiers, needed a little time to fully settle into his new way of life in Aldershot. Although he appreciated that it was necessary, he found endless marching and bayonet drills mundane and physically taxing. He would much rather have been on the golf course or in the gym. Thankfully, having his five other boxing pals for company made the days pass more quickly.

As well as learning the basics of army life at Aldershot barracks, Wilde had also been given an opportunity to branch out into silent film.

---

79 *South Wales Weekly Post* 20 January 1917

A Pit Boy's Romance, which was directed by A.E. Coleby and Arthur Rooke, told the story of a teenage couple from a tiny Welsh mining village. Wilde plays Jimmy Davies, a promising up-and-coming boxer. His sweetheart, Mifanwy Griffiths, dreams of being a famous actress and runs away to London seeking fame and fortune. Unfortunately for her, Laurie Ayers, the manager of the dramatics company where Mifanwy is now acting, takes a liking to her. When Mifanwy finds out about Ayers's amorous intentions, she runs away and finds work as a flower girl. By coincidence, Jimmy is in London training for a fight against a top American (played by Tommy Noble).

Knowing that his sweetheart is in London, Jimmy frantically searches for her. Eventually, he manages to find her. It turns out that Mifanwy has been lured to Ayers's flat under false pretences. However, finding Mifanwy has taken so long that Jimmy is now late for his big fight at the National Sporting Club. Somehow, Jimmy manages to arrive in the ring just in the nick of time and goes on to soundly defeat the American who, it transpires, Ayers has backed with every penny he has. With Ayers financially ruined, Jimmy and Mifanwy are reunited in a loving embrace in the centre of the ring as Jimmy is announced the winner.

A Pit Boy's Romance was a good project for Wilde. It was totally different from anything he had done before and required plenty of application and concentration. Although it was never going to win any awards, Wilde had a great time putting the film together and he especially enjoyed the company of former opponent Tommy Noble, as well as the other members of the cast and crew. Much to Wilde's delight, the film was well received when it was released in cinemas. It was shown nightly all over the country throughout 1917.

On 12 March 1917, Wilde defended his British title against George Clark at the National Sporting Club.

Clark was no stranger to Wilde. Nineteen months earlier, Wilde had soundly beaten him in eight rounds. However, two wins over Alf Mansfield and Sid Smith, albeit at bantamweight, had reignited Clark's career.

The only sticking point for Bettinson and the committee at the NSC during purse negotiations was whether Clark would be able to shed 6lb in weight. Clark and his manager assured Bettinson that he could.

Clark had been comprehensively beaten in his first fight with Wilde, for which Clark had weighed 8st 4lb. Now, by agreeing to boil himself down to 8st, Clark, who no doubt would be severely weakened after having to lose nearly half a stone, was handing Wilde an even bigger advantage.

The only hope that Clark had this time was that Wilde was having to fit his boxing training around army drills rather than being able to concentrate solely on preparing for the fight. Maybe Wilde would come in slightly undercooked? It was unlikely, but not impossible.

Clark, it transpired, had tremendous difficulty getting down to the required weight. He looked pale and drawn at the weigh-in and had to strip naked to tip the scales at 8st even. Wilde took to the scales in his army uniform and was still only 6st 12lb.

The odds on the man from Lambeth causing an upset were 5/1 and those odds seemed to be totally justified when the first bell rang.

Wilde was in total command from early on. After a cagey opening round in which there were few scoring punches, Wilde took charge in the second. Double jabs and follow-up rights repeatedly thudded into Clark's face and, when he tried to throw punches back, he found himself swiping at thin air.

In the third round, Wilde's right hands started to snap Clark's head back. Two hard smashes to Clark's weight-drained body caused him to wince and hang on, earning him a stern warning from the referee. It was becoming obvious to all those watching that Clark would not last much longer.

Wilde came out firing in the fourth, determined to get the fight over and done with. Rapid lefts and rights to Clark's body doubled him over. Wilde tagged him with a left hook on the chin as he was falling. Clark, in obvious distress, looked over to his corner. He rose at eight, but was met with a fusillade of body shots that forced him to take another eight count. Somehow, Clark, who was as weak as a kitten, got to his feet. Wilde unleashed lefts and rights to Clark's head and body. A right to the jaw floored Clark for a third time. As Clark lay on the canvas, his corner threw in the towel just as the referee, J.H. Douglas, counted to four.

The National Sporting Club erupted when 'Peggy' Bettinson announced Wilde as the winner and an even louder roar went up when Bettinson told the crowd that Wilde had now won the Lord Lonsdale challenge belt outright.

Just ten days later, Wilde was back in the ring again. This time he was topping a five-fight bill in a one-off British Army versus Canadian Army event at Holborn Stadium.

Wilde took on Private Frankie Russell in a fight that had optimistically been scheduled for 15 rounds. However, it was apparent after the first minute of the contest that the Canadian was way out of his depth. Russell was knocked down three times in the second round by straight lefts and four times in the third before the referee stopped the bout.

The British Army went on to win by five bouts to nil. As Wilde celebrated with his fellow soldiers later that afternoon, he could not possibly have foreseen that he would not fight competitively again for 13 months.

Despite being the British and world flyweight champion, by the spring of 1917 Wilde's career was in something of a stalemate. He had beaten all the top flyweights of his era – Sid Smith, Joe Symonds, Tancy Lee, Alf Mansfield and Tommy Noble, not to mention the best that America had at that time in Young Zulu Kid.

Domestically, there was a paucity of suitable challengers for Wilde at 8st. All of the past flyweight champions were now fighting at bantamweight and *Boxing* could see no other option for Wilde other than to join them, even though he still struggled to weigh more than 6st 12lb.

At least Wilde's win over Young Zulu Kid had got the Americans more interested in him. Several American managers had sent cables to *Boxing* claiming that they had the fighter who could beat Wilde, providing the money was right. Joe Burman, according to his manager, was a fearsome eight-stoner from Chicago, while Larney Lichtenstein, the manager of Artie Simons from New Orleans, told *Boxing* he was willing to 'bet everything I possess, including our end of the purse, that Mr Wilde cannot beat my aspirant for the world's flyweight title'.[80]

Midway through May, Wilde ruptured his stomach while on bayonet practice and had to spend a week in hospital. At first, it was thought he would have to have an operation but, after a week of bed rest, he was fit enough to return to the barracks. With his health restored, Wilde passed the instructor's course and, by July 1917, he had been transferred to Sandhurst where his superior officer was none other than Capt. John Hopley, a man who had not only earned a boxing 'blue' at Cambridge but had also represented MCC at cricket.

Jimmy settled in well at Sandhurst. He found the environment more relaxed than he had anticipated and he was extremely popular with everyone. He especially enjoyed sparring with the young officers. Under Wilde's tutelage, the boxing team improved beyond measure. Nothing pleased Wilde more than seeing the men he had trained emerge victorious from their inter-services matches.

The physical training was all-consuming and there was a great feeling of team spirit at Sandhurst. There were many light-hearted moments and acts of high jinx, but the dark clouds of war still invaded the mind during quiet times.

80 *Boxing* 25 April 1917

'They were good, keen fellows all of them,' Wilde would remember. 'They seemed to have only one objective; the battlefront. There were times when I envied them, and others when I told myself not to be a fool. The war had lasted too long for anyone to imagine it was going to be a picnic. I wonder if a single soldier, after two years of conflict, honestly ached to go overseas. They were not irresponsible boys. For their age, many of them were weighed down too heavily by a sense of responsibility.'[81]

When it was announced that Southwark's Dick Heasman was going to challenge Wilde for his Lonsdale belt on 29 April 1918 at the National Sporting Club, there was widespread surprise among many in the boxing fraternity. Heasman had only been boxing professionally for ten months and it seems that two 15-round points wins at the NSC against two Welshmen, Tommy Davis and Tal Jones, had convinced 'Peggy' Bettinson that Heasman would put up a good fight against Wilde.

Bettinson, who was normally such a good judge of a fighter's capabilities, was no doubt cajoled into making the match by Heasman's manager, Alf Hewitt, who was convinced that his man, having recently beaten two Welshmen, could now make Wilde a third.

For Heasman, fighting Wilde, let alone beating him, was a totally different proposition to outpointing Davis and Jones, two fighters who were nowhere near Wilde's class. What is more, although he was a pretty boxer with a good jab, Heasman could not crack an egg with his punch.

---

81 Jimmy Wilde *Fighting Was My Business* p.135

Boxing's main concern was whether Wilde would be as fighting fit as he had been before joining up. They were worried that, although he may still have his 'wind', he may have lost some of his sharpness after being inactive, except for exhibitions, for just over a year. There is no doubt that Hewitt and Heasman were hoping that he had. *Boxing*, quite correctly, believed Heasman was being rushed and could have done with another two or three years of experience before going in with someone of Wilde's calibre.

At the weigh-in, Wilde was 7st 2lb and looked a picture of health. As *Boxing* had predicted, army life had indeed added a little more muscle to his still slender frame. Heasman, on the other hand, came in half an ounce over the agreed weight limit of 7st 4lb. Wilde was unmoved.

'It doesn't matter if he weighs a ton, it's all right,' he said.

Bettinson, however, was insistent. Heasman was contractually obliged to come in at the agreed weight and he had to take himself off to the steam bath and weigh in again. Wilde already had the fight won.

Later that night, as the two boxers were introduced, Wilde looked confident and relaxed while Heasman looked as if he was on his way to the gallows.

Wilde came out in the first with his hands placed just above his hips, swaying left and right. Every time Wilde feinted to throw a punch, Heasman flinched in an exaggerated manner. After a minute of feeling each other out, Wilde connected with a solid right that drove Heasman back to the ropes. Another hard right made him totter sideways. Wilde feinted with his left, then threw a lightning fast right that put Heasman over. The Londoner got up at two and back-pedalled, but Wilde strode after him. Another right to the jaw put Heasman over for a six count. When Heasman was floored for a third time, unluckily for him, the bell saved him.

As the bell rang for the second round, many in the hall were already getting ready to leave. A solid left-right put Heasman down. After listening to the referee count to eight, Heasman dragged his weary body upright. A light left to the face made Heasman stumble back on his heels. Just as Wilde was getting ready to throw another left-right combination, the towel from Heasman's corner came flying into the ring.

Those who had made it known in the preceding weeks that the fight had come too soon for Heasman had been proved right. He had been totally outclassed in three minutes and 58 seconds. Heasman's manager, Hewitt – who had told all and sundry that Heasman could beat Wilde – and Bettinson were totally to blame for allowing such a mismatch to take place. Hewitt's judgement of both his own man and of Wilde had been way off the mark and it had been his fighter who had suffered in a fight that *Boxing* called 'a crime'.[82]

After beating Heasman, Wilde returned to Sandhurst where he carried on with his duties as a physical training instructor, as well as taking part in exhibition matches to raise money for the Sportsmen's Ambulance Fund. Although Heasman had not put

82 *Boxing* 30 April 1918

up much resistance, it had been good to be back in the familiar surroundings of the National Sporting Club.

In early August 1918, alongside the river Somme at Amiens in northern France, the Allied forces launched what would later be known as the 'Hundred Day Offensive' in a battle that would ultimately lead to the armistice.

To help raise money for the Wounded Soldiers Fund, Jack Callaghan and co-promoter Jerry Cripps matched Wilde with featherweight Joe Conn at Stamford Bridge football ground on 31 August.

Conn, who was from Bow in east London, had his first recorded fight in 1911 when he outpointed Nipper Barton after six rounds at the Judean Boxing Club in Whitechapel.

Fighting mainly at the Ring in Blackfriars, Conn fought twice, sometimes three times a month over the next five years. For 12 months from the summer of 1917, Conn hit something of a purple patch in his career, beating Tommy Noble on points after 20 rounds, Sid Smith with a fourth-round knockout, Billy Fry on points after 20, Idris Jones by knockout in the ninth and Curly Walker on points in a 15-rounder. This run of impressive wins had earned him a shot at Tancy Lee, who was now the British featherweight champion.

As soon as the fight was announced, the newspapers were unanimously of the opinion that Conn was taking a huge risk. If he lost to Wilde, who was 2st lighter, then not only would his reputation be severely dented, but the validity of his upcoming challenge for Lee's title in two months' time would be seriously questioned. 'Peggy' Bettinson assured everyone that Conn had earned the right to fight Lee for the Lonsdale belt and would be doing so, whatever the result against Wilde.

When the military sports bodies got wind of the fight, they let it be known that they were firmly against it taking place. There were going to be serving soldiers on the bill who were going to get paid, which went against the spirit of sport for those who were in the forces. Those who were serving their country were expected to participate in their chosen sport for recreation or to raise money for appointed charities, not to profit personally. Callaghan, in an attempt to appease, announced that a large percentage of the gate receipts would be donated to the War Fund.

The *London Weekly Dispatch* wrote that it was 'ridiculous to think that Wilde and Conn can put in a month of hard training and still give their full attention to their military duties'. The editor of *Boxing* was quick to point out that Wilde's boxing had never interfered with his job at Sandhurst and that Conn worked in a reserved occupation.[83]

As the fight drew nearer, Wilde's £2,000 purse was creating a headache for Callaghan and Cripps. Shortly after Wilde's last fight against Dick Heasman, the Imperial Services Boxing Association (ISBA) brought in a rule stating that serving boxers were no longer allowed to fight for money.

The ISBA promptly told Callaghan that Wilde was not to receive any money for fighting Conn. Instead, he should be presented with a cup or a medal. Callaghan promised that he

83 *London Weekly Dispatch* 4 August 1918

would comply with these rules and attempted to calm the waters further by announcing that 500 wounded soldiers would be allowed in free of charge. A couple of days later, after further criticism by the press, Callaghan upped the figure to 2,000.

Amid all this consternation, Wilde got down to training at Sandhurst. Four Welsh featherweights – George Hatto, Idris Jones, Young Charles and Billy Fry – were given instructions to manhandle Wilde in sparring so that he grew accustomed to being up against the extra weight. Fry and Jones, who had boxed 45 rounds with Conn between them, were an invaluable help.

The terms of the contest had strictly stated that Conn must be 9st or under on the morning of the weigh-in. Conn came in at 8st 13½lb. Wilde, who weighed 7st 2lb, was giving away a massive 25½lb.

At 4pm, both boxers made their way from the dressing rooms to the ring that had been erected in the centre circle of the Stamford Bridge pitch. The local constabulary were on strike, so Callaghan and Cripps had to arrange for several hundred men from nearby military hospitals to guard the ring. It was just another obstacle to overcome for the promoters in an event that had been beset by problems from the very start.

In the first round, Conn (54-15-6) stood upright while Wilde came out in a slight crouch which made Conn's four-inch height advantage seem even greater. Wilde just shaded the round when, near the end, he landed a good right on Conn's jaw that drew an 'Ooh!' from the crowd.

During the second and third rounds, Wilde tried to draw Conn in by feinting and shuffling. Neither did much, though, as they both sparred for openings. Conn opened up a bit more in the fourth and fifth, but Wilde made him miss by slipping most of the punches.

As they came out for the sixth, Conn made Wilde's lip bleed with a heavy left jab. Although Conn's jabs were infrequent, they were heavy and, in the seventh and eighth, he started to score with his right cross. As the bell rang to end the round, Wilde slumped down on his stool, breathing heavily.

In the ninth, Conn reopened a slight nick over Wilde's left eye that he had picked up in sparring. Wilde was unperturbed and shook Conn with a thudding right to even up a quiet round.

As the bell rang for the tenth, the fight was still evenly poised. This all changed, however, when Conn missed with a left. He was wide open to a counter-right from Wilde that put him over. Conn got up at nine. Wilde tore after him. Conn was floored four more times before the end of the round.

In the 11th, Wilde rained in blows to Conn's head and body, forcing him to the boards on three occasions. As the bell went, Conn wearily tottered back to his corner.

The 12th round was the last. Conn covered up as Wilde threw everything at him with both hands. Conn was knocked down four times in quick succession. Gamely, Conn picked himself up off his hands and knees and rose to his feet, only to be floored again. This time the referee, J.T. Hulls, waved the fight over.

One massive right hand from Wilde in the tenth had taken everything out of Conn and had completely changed the fight. It was some feat by Wilde against a man who, two months later, was going to challenge for the British featherweight title. *Boxing* called it Wilde's 'greatest triumph' and asked its readers if there was anybody out there who could beat him.[84]

Although the weather had been fair, the attendance had been disappointing. The stands were sparsely populated and *Boxing* estimated that the crowd had been around the 7,500 mark. It was well below the 30,000 Callaghan and Cripps had hoped for.

Now Callaghan and Cripps had to get around the problem regarding Wilde's purse. At the after-fight banquet later that evening, which was held at the Eccentric Club in London, Bernard Oppenheimer, the famous diamond merchant, presented Jimmy and Elizabeth with a small packet of diamonds worth £2,000. Oppenheimer discreetly advised Jimmy to exchange them for cash at a reputable jewellers as soon as possible.

Although the ISBA did not know about the diamonds, it had taken a dim view of the fact that, initially, Wilde was due to be paid to fight Conn. The only reason he hadn't been was because the ISBA had intervened.

On 2 September 1918, the ISBA convened a meeting in London and decided that professional boxers who were in the forces would not be allowed to fight on professional promotions until the war had ended. Members of the armed forces could

84 *Boxing* 4 September 1918

only box in inter-services tournaments or in exhibitions to raise money for the War Fund.

Shortly after being told about the new rule, Wilde announced that he did not want a repeat of the Conn affair and that he was temporarily retiring from boxing and would only return to the ring when the war was over.

It seemed that Wilde could not stay out of the news. On 8 September 1918, the *News of the World* reported that: 'On the train journey back to Wales, a loud brute got on the train and sat in the same carriage as Wilde. Jimmy asked the man, who was constantly swearing, to mind his language as there were ladies present along with a member of the clergy, no less. When the train stopped, the man, who was said to be four times bigger than Wilde, waited on the platform for him. When Wilde got off the train, the lout swung his right fist at him. Wilde deftly slipped the swing and knocked the oaf out with a right hand of his own! It is reported that it took 20 minutes for the ruffian to come round. The following day, Wilde received a letter from the clergyman saying: "I have always admired Wilde as a boxer, but now, more importantly, I admire him as a man."'

16

Fighting The Allies

ON 11 November 1918, the Great War finally came to an end. It is estimated that in the region of 35,000 Welsh soldiers were killed during the conflict. Eighty-four of those brave men came from Tylorstown.

The following day, Prime Minister David Lloyd George published a message in the *Western Mail*: 'What can I say more than that the cause of righteousness has triumphed and the freedom of the small nations of the world has been won and established forever. I am proud to think that my own little nation of Wales has borne its full share of the task of winning this great triumph.'

To acknowledge the important role boxing had played in the services during the war and to raise money for the Prisoners of War Fund, the ISBA arranged a two-day exhibition tournament at the Royal Albert Hall on 11 and 12 December.

The Allied Services King's Trophy was made up of boxers who had served in the army, navy and air force for Britain, America, Australia, New Zealand, South Africa and Canada. Each of the eight weight divisions were represented, with eight boxers in each division who would fight quarter-finals, semi-finals and a final. Points were awarded for each victory, with the country with the most points after two days of competition receiving the trophy.

Each bout was three rounds in duration. The first two rounds were two minutes long, with the final round being three minutes. Commissioned officers were assigned the task of judging and refereeing the bouts and, in an attempt to even up the contests between those who had boxed as amateurs and those who were professionals, larger 12oz gloves were worn.

On the opening afternoon of the tournament, exuberant patriotism oozed from every part of the Royal Albert Hall. Admiral Sir David Beatty, Commander of the Grand Fleet, tried to quietly take his seat near the ring, but the 10,000 in attendance stamped their feet in unison shouting 'Speech! Speech!' Reluctantly, Beatty climbed into the ring. 'This is not the time for speech-making. This is the time for fighting. I came here today to see the finest exponents of boxing which can be produced by the Anglo-Saxon race. They say that the war is over and talking has begun. Therefore, I had better get down.' Beatty climbed out of the ring and took his seat amid deafening cheers and applause.[85]

It would have seemed natural for Wilde, who weighed 7st 2lb, to have entered the tournament in the flyweight group. There is no doubt that, had he done so, he would have won it with ease, as all of the servicemen in that weight class were nothing more

85 *Sporting Life* 12 December 1918

than enthusiastic amateurs. The bantamweight group, however, was far more appealing to him due to the participation of two top Americans – Pal Moore and Joe Lynch.

Pal Moore was born in 1894 in Memphis, Tennessee. He made his professional debut in 1913 and made rapid progress through the bantamweight ranks, despite most of his fights being 'no decision' affairs.

Moore really came to prominence in October 1915 when he took on the world bantamweight champion Kid Williams in an eight-round 'no decision' bout at the Phoenix Athletic Club. Boxing beautifully, Moore floored Williams twice during the bout. The ringside reporters awarded Moore the newspaper decision. Because Moore had given him such a tough fight, Kid Williams never gave him the chance to fight for his title.

One month later, Moore showed his class by outpointing the future world bantamweight champion Pete Herman, as well as losing to and then beating the equally talented Joe Lynch. By the time he arrived in London, Moore was considered to be the best bantamweight never to have fought for the world title.

Joe Lynch was born in New York City in 1898 and turned professional at the age of 17. Standing 5ft 7½in, Lynch was unusually tall for a bantamweight, but his beanpole-like figure hid a wiry strength.

Lynch had fought everyone of note – mostly in 'no decision' bouts – by the time he was called up by the US Army. Jackie Sharkey, Johnny Ertle, Kid Williams and Pete Herman were just some of the top-class men he had shared a ring with.

By the winter of 1918, Lynch and Moore were the top two contenders for Pete Herman's world bantamweight crown.

It is a mark of the high esteem in which Wilde was held that, even though he was in a group including two top Americans and would be conceding around 18lb in weight to each, he was still considered the favourite to win the bantamweight group when the ISBA made the draw.

Pal Moore (US Navy) v Seaman Patten (Royal Navy)
Johnny Hughes (RAF) v G.F. Benson (New Zealand)
Jimmy Wilde (Army) v Joe Lynch (US Army)
Albert Evans (Australia) v J. Jones (Canada)

Wilde and Lynch received a raucous reception when they climbed into the ring on the first afternoon. Lynch towered over Wilde as the referee bought them together in the centre of the ring for their final instructions.

As expected, the fight was fast-paced. Wilde came out aggressively and caught Lynch with a few left jabs before moving out of range. Lynch came out for the second with a little more purpose and started to score with his left jab. Encouraged by his success, Lynch threw a left that Wilde slipped. Wilde shot a right counter over Lynch's outstretched left arm and connected squarely on the American's chin, pushing him off balance and causing him to topple over. There is no doubt that, had the boxers been wearing smaller gloves, the punch would have done a lot more damage. Lynch, slightly embarrassed, quickly jumped up and tried a big right to Wilde's jaw, which was neatly parried away.

Lynch was two rounds down going into the last. Rather than force the pace, Lynch decided it would be wiser to counter on the back foot. Wilde was still too fast for him. Every time Lynch drew him in, Wilde connected with a left-right combination and darted away, leaving Lynch swiping at thin air. After seven minutes of frantic action, all three judges agreed that Wilde had won every round.

Within a few hours, Wilde was back in the ring for his semi-final bout against the Australian soldier Albert 'Digger' Evans, a 23-year-old southpaw from Cobar in New South Wales.

Even though he had only been boxing for a short while, 'Digger' was not lacking in confidence – unlike the crowd, who feared for his safety. The Aussie continually scored with straight right leads which had Wilde so confused that halfway through the round he turned southpaw himself in an effort to land a telling blow.

Wilde started to have a little more success in the second with his left jabs. He stayed orthodox throughout and, although a great deal of missing was done by both, Wilde edged the round on his greater workrate.

Evans was exhausted as the bell sounded to start the third. Wilde threw some fast flurries and made Evans chase after him. Wilde won by two rounds to one.

In the other half of the draw, Pal Moore had fought his way through to the final by easily outpointing Seaman Patten and Johnny Hughes to set up the final everyone wanted to see.

For the 10,000 people packed into the Royal Albert Hall on the final night of the competition, Wilde's fight against Moore was the most anticipated of the eight finals, with the all-British heavyweight clash between Bombardier Billy Wells and Joe Beckett not far behind it.

When Pal Moore took off his dressing gown in the ring, the disparity in size between himself and Wilde became starkly obvious. Moore had weighed 8st 6lb on the morning before the tournament started, but by the Thursday evening *Boxing* strongly suspected that he was 9st or possibly even a few pounds heavier. Up until now, Wilde had been the favourite, but some in the crowd were having second thoughts as the two fighters were introduced.

Both boxers started cautiously. The few punches that were thrown in the first were either slipped or blocked. In such a short contest, it seemed that neither man wanted to commit themselves and make the first mistake.

Wilde was the first to take the initiative in the second. A rapid left-right-left-right scored and Wilde had skipped out of range by the time Moore could retaliate. Eventually, Moore managed to land an ill-timed left jab which hit Wilde in the throat. Whether Moore paused in order to apologise or was simply shocked that he had landed a worthwhile punch will never be known, but he stepped back and failed to follow up. That short pause was all the time Wilde needed to gather himself and score with two sharp lefts.

In the second half of the round, Moore tried to use his

superior weight to his advantage by leaning on Wilde, but Jimmy was clever on the inside and worked over Moore's body with lefts and rights. A right uppercut that lifted the American's head up and back, just as the bell sounded, secured the round for Wilde.

As the bell clanged for the third and final round, everyone in the hall – barring the Americans – were of the opinion that Moore needed a stoppage to win. Wilde scored with a left and a right. Moore was still reluctant to attack. With only a minute-and-a-half left, Moore must have realised it was now or never and went after Wilde with both hands in a desperate attempt to get a knockout. Wilde took a fair few punches, but he also ducked and swayed out of the way of a good many of the blows, with Moore forced to hold until the bell rang.

As the two boxers embraced in the ring, Wilde beamed with joy. Moore, on the other hand, looked weary and resigned to the fact that he had lost. The master of ceremonies, Lt. Col. J. Parkin, picked up his loud hailer and waved his left hand up and down for silence. 'The winner – Chief Petty Officer Moore.'

Wilde stood in his corner looking shocked and bemused. Moore, on hearing the announcement, started jumping up and down deliriously. Even his cornermen were loath to join in with his celebrations. They looked totally embarrassed by it all.

Wilde, a true sportsman, walked over to the American's corner and shook Pal's hand, at which point boos turned into loud howls of derision. The incensed crowd demanded that the verdict be overturned. At the back of the hall, scuffling broke out between the British and the Americans.

The MC, Parkin, pleaded for order, but was ignored. A full-scale riot was breaking out. Wilde and Moore were quickly ushered out of the ring. Colonel Ronald Campbell, the director of army physical training, was so fearful that the rest of the tournament would be ruined that he gave up trying to subdue the crowd and sent for Jim Driscoll instead.

'Peerless' Jim climbed through the ropes and took the loud hailer. 'Ladies and gentlemen. As trainer of the British Army team I am quite satisfied with the decision of the judges and, may I say, so is Wilde.'

More boos and shouts of 'robbery' followed as Driscoll, who did not really believe himself that Moore had won, got out of the ring. Thankfully, King George V, who had stayed away with a cold, was not in attendance to witness such a fracas.

Eventually, it was MC Parkin and a vocal member of the crowd who inadvertently managed to restore order. Parkin took his cap, placed it on his head and stood to attention in front of the royal box, which was patronised by Prince Albert. As Parkin prepared to salute the prince, the vocal man in the crowd shouted 'One! Two!' which made a large section of the crowd burst into spontaneous laughter.

That one moment seemed to drain all of the bitterness out of the hall. Once the laughter had subsided, a normal chattering din took hold and the two featherweights who had been held up while all this was going on were able to make their way to the ring.

Poor MC Parkin had to introduce another six bouts that evening after the Wilde fiasco and he was on the receiving end of the crowd's crude humour every time he stepped into the ring.

It was all very unfortunate for the ISBA. It had put on a well-organised festival of boxing which had provided great entertainment over two days, yet it had been overshadowed by an appalling decision in the tournament's most high-profile bout.[86]

The following week, *Boxing* was scathing of the three judges. 'Nine hundred and ninety-seven who saw the contest knew Wilde had won. It was one of the clearest-cut contests of the whole tournament.'[87]

For Wilde, it was immensely frustrating. What made it worse was the fact that Moore did not show any contrition about the verdict. He was more confident than ever that he could beat Wilde, especially if they fought over a longer distance and wore smaller gloves.

As far as the hard-bitten boxing promoters on both sides of the Atlantic were concerned, the controversy over the decision, even if it had been in an exhibition bout, was manna from heaven. They were already thinking about the possibility of a money-spinning rematch.

86 The British Army won the King's trophy. The runners-up were the US Army.
87 *Boxing* 16 December 1918

17

A Controversy Avenged

IN JANUARY 1919, Joe Lynch came back to England. 'Peggy' Bettinson and the committee at the NSC had signed him up to fight Tommy Noble and then have a return match with Wilde.

Noble, who had won the vacant British bantamweight title after Joe Fox had relinquished the belt because he could no longer make the weight, was expected to be a stern test for the American. Many boxing insiders were keen to find out just how good Lynch really was after his brief showing against Wilde at the Albert Hall.

Both men had agreed to fight at 8st 8lb. Lynch made the weight, but Noble had to pay a £25 forfeit when he refused to get on the scales. Reporters claimed he was nearer to 9st.

A much-anticipated fight turned out to be something of a damp squib. Noble had done himself no favours at all in coming into the ring so heavy and he was lacklustre throughout. Despite this, Lynch refused to press home his advantage. The New Yorker was ultra-cautious and content to pile up points with his left jab and box his way to a drab points win.

Bettinson was not deterred by the poor showing. He had hoped that Noble would have drawn the best out of Lynch, but the Londoner had shown no inclination to mix it. Wilde, who had been watching from ringside, was confident that he could beat Lynch. A three-round exhibition bout with large padded gloves had not proved much. A 15-round fight with 6oz gloves would be a totally different spectacle.

For the first time in two years, Jimmy was able to train at home in Tylorstown. The facilities at Sandhurst had been top class but, even so, there was no place like home. Light sparring with Billy Fry, roadwork – with Elizabeth beside him on her bicycle – and a couple of rounds of golf every day with Benny Williams made up Wilde's training regime.

Lynch based himself at Windsor in Berkshire. Alongside his cornerman, the American middleweight Eddie McGoorty, Lynch kept in shape by sparring with the former British champion Sid Smith and Tommy Gardner, a tough featherweight from Smethwick in the West Midlands.

Like many, Lynch had been disappointed with his performance against Noble. A couple of weeks before his fight with Wilde, he told *Boxing* that 'fighting Jimmy will be a lot tougher than fighting Noble' and that, with the fight being over a longer distance, it 'would be a fairer gauge of each man's capabilities'. Lynch had worked himself into great shape at Windsor and said that 'win, lose or draw I expect to get a fair deal from the referee and fully expect to go back to the States victorious'.[88]

---

88 *Boxing* 12 March 1919

Boxing was right in saying that Lynch 'was the most talented boxer that Wilde had stepped into the ring with so far'. Once again they were siding with Wilde but were hedging their bets slightly because they knew that, by the time he got in the ring, Lynch would be two or three pounds over the 8st 6lb limit which he had weighed in at earlier in the afternoon, giving the American an advantage of between 18 and 21lb.[89]

The trade paper predicted that Wilde would start fast, make Lynch miss and then overwhelm the bigger man with hard counters that would force a late stoppage. Lynch's best chance of victory was to tie up Wilde, lean on him and hope that the extra weight would wear him down.

On the evening of 31 March 1919, Wilde and Lynch climbed into the ring at a packed and expectant National Sporting Club. After giving both fighters their instructions, the referee, John H. Douglas, stepped out of the ring and proceeded to take his place on his raised platform on the other side of the ropes, as was the time-honoured rule at boxing's headquarters.

From the first bell, Lynch gave ground, allowing Wilde to charge after him, at which point Lynch would tie up Wilde and duck low until the referee broke them apart. Both sparred warily in the second and third and only really engaged when they were at close quarters.

From round four through to the end of the seventh, Wilde continued to take the fight to Lynch, who was being as cautious as he had been against Noble. In his corner, Eddie McGoorty, who

89 *Boxing* 26 March 1919

had a reputation as a safety-first fighter, repeatedly told Lynch to watch out for Wilde's right hand. Lynch was clearly boxing to instruction. Do not lead off first. Let Wilde come in and then counter if possible or, better still, clinch.

The American continued to grapple with Wilde at every opportunity as the bout progressed and was warned several times by Douglas for kidney punching. Wilde was looking tired by the tenth. Lynch's punches around the back were draining Wilde, but Lynch was unwilling to commit himself to a sustained burst of punching and constantly surrendered the initiative.

Every time Lynch ducked low, Wilde would try to get an uppercut to land, but few of them were able to get through. In the 11th, Lynch decided to open up and whaled away at Jimmy. Most of the punches hit Wilde on the back and he was forced to rest on one knee after a particularly hard combination around the kidney area. Douglas declined to count or warn Lynch, who sportingly outstretched his arm to help Jimmy up, which drew applause from the crowd.

For the next four rounds, Lynch doggedly stuck to his gameplan of holding and retreating. Not once did he make his significant height and reach advantage count. On more than one occasion, he had the chance to keep Wilde on the end of his long jab, but he was so mindful of being caught with one of Wilde's devastating right hands that he would immediately go back on the defensive. Such negative tactics had cost Lynch the fight. As the bell rang to end the fight, Douglas had no hesitation in raising Wilde's arm.

Jimmy's fight against Lynch had not been a typical Wilde fight by any means. It had been a stop-start, frustrating affair which had been difficult to score due to Lynch's willingness to hold and smother at every opportunity. Wilde had secured the verdict simply because he had gone forward and made the fight.

If Lynch had been aware of how tired Wilde actually was, then the result could well have been different. Jimmy sat on his stool exhausted at the end of the bout and it took an almighty effort for him to stand when the Prince of Wales climbed into the ring to congratulate him.

The crowd at the NSC had been as perplexed by Lynch's tactics as Wilde had been. After the fight, Wilde asked Lynch:

'Why didn't you open up, Joe?'

'Well, I'm mighty pleased with what I've done,' Lynch replied. 'McGoorty told me to keep away from you and I think that was wise. Sure, I'm pleased to have stayed as long as I did with you.'[90]

The following week, *Boxing* was succinct and direct in summarising the American's effort. 'Lynch's main aim was to avoid being knocked out. His fear of defeat was greater than his desire for victory.'[91]

After returning home, Wilde took it easy for a few days. His back was bruised from Lynch's punches and his kidneys were giving him particular discomfort.

Boxing was in agreement with Teddy Lewis that, when

---

90 Jimmy Wilde *Fighting Was My Business* p.150
91 *Boxing* 9 April 1919

fighting bantamweights in the future, Wilde's opponent would have to weigh in at ringside moments before the first bell. Wilde had conceded 18lb to Lynch at the 2pm weigh-in and Lewis strongly suspected the American had put on an extra two or three pounds by the time the fight started that evening.

Nowadays, Wilde would not have fought for at least another six months. Back in 1919, boxing was very different. Just three weeks after his gruelling encounter with Lynch, Wilde was back at Pudsey Street in Liverpool fighting Castleford's Jimmy Buck.

Despite being unbeaten, Buck was nowhere near Wilde's class. The main reason Wilde had been booked to appear was because the Liverpool Sporting Syndicate was keen to cash in on his victory over Lynch. Having Wilde on the bill guaranteed the promoters a bumper turnout and, with it, large gate receipts.

Wilde being 'served up one of the juiciest lemons of his career' was how *Boxing* described the fight. Buck came out swinging but he was repeatedly knocked off balance by Wilde's stinging left jab in the first. A left-right put Buck over in the second, forcing him to take an eight count, and he was on unsteady legs as he went back to his corner. Things got worse for Buck in the third and fourth rounds as Wilde peppered him with lefts and rights from all angles. Groggy and bloody, Buck was a sitting target for Wilde in the fifth and was floored heavily three times by right hands before the referee, Tom Gamble, stopped the fight.[92]

92 *Boxing* 23 April 1919

The syndicate was surprised and disappointed with the low attendance. Before the fight, it had anticipated a large crowd and had persuaded Wilde to take a percentage of the gate receipts instead of a set purse. This turned out to be a mistake. The Pudsey Street fight crowd knew their boxing and, not prepared to pay high prices to witness such a mismatch, locals fans stayed away, resulting in Wilde receiving an unusually low purse.

Alf Mansfield, the old campaigner from Aldgate, had been hankering for a third fight with Wilde since they had last met in 1914. Alf, who was coming towards the end of a long, arduous career, was granted his wish at Holborn Stadium on 16 May.

Many boxing writers considered it unwise for Mansfield (53-44-21) to take the fight. He had always taken two punches in order to land one of his own and had been complaining of eyesight problems for the past two years. One thing was certain about Mansfield. He would give everything he had once the bell rang. Jimmy had always had tremendous admiration for him. He was, without doubt, one of the most durable men in British boxing during the first 20 years of the 20th century.

At the start of the fight, Mansfield (8st 4lb) came out throwing fierce combinations which Wilde avoided by swaying and shuffling out of the way. Alf was fighting like a whirling dervish and carried on throwing caution to the wind throughout the following four rounds. By the end of the sixth, Mansfield's face was beginning to mark up.

Despite the fast pace of the fight, Wilde (7st 2lb) was boxing well within himself. Underneath the hot ring lights, he was ice cold. Mansfield took an awful amount of punishment from the ninth through to the end of the 12th. He was just too brave for his own good.

In the 13th, Wilde sensed that Mansfield was there for the taking. A left jab, which jolted back Mansfield's head, was followed by a smashing right that put the Londoner down for a nine count. Mansfield got up, only to be put down for the same amount of time again after taking another left-right on the jaw. Mansfield shook his head from side to side, trying to shake away the grogginess. Somehow, he managed to drag himself upright. The end was brutal. Wilde feinted, landed a left and then knocked Mansfield out cold with a follow-up right cross. As Alf lay unconscious on his back with the referee, Eugene Corri, counting over him, Alf's corner belatedly threw a white towel into the ring.[93]

Since the previous December, Teddy Lewis and promoter C.B. Cochran had been working towards a return fight with Pal Moore. It was a fight that everyone wanted to see and Wilde was desperate to have the chance to put the record straight.

Setting the terms for the fight had not been easy. After the King's Trophy, Moore had returned to America and fought 15 'no decision' bouts in six months. He had gone the distance with Pete Herman in March and Jackie Sharkey in Wisconsin shortly before setting sail for England.

Moore's backers had been unwilling to come to England at first. They wanted Wilde to travel over to America. Had Wilde

93 Mansfield retired the following year. He had fought Wilde while blind in one eye and within eight years was totally blind. His wife, who was a music hall star, gave up her career to look after him and help him run his sweet and tobacco shop in Peckham.

done so, there would have been little money in it for either man. The bantamweights found it impossible to draw big money in the States. By coming to London, however, Moore was guaranteed the biggest payday of his career. Eventually, Moore's manager, Nate Lewis, relented when Cochran offered £3,000 to the winner and £2,000 to the loser.

For Cochran, it was a major coup. 'It will be a great night at Olympia on 17 July,' he told the *Daily Mirror*. 'I believe we shall have a record American attendance. Many are making the journey over to England expressly to see Moore fight our wonderful little champion.'[94]

Cochran's confidence was not misplaced. Tickets, which were priced from five shillings to £10, were selling well and it looked likely that the Olympia, which had a capacity of 20,000, would see a sell-out.

Moore arrived in England at the end of June and set up his training camp at the Abercorn Arms in Stanmore. The old warhorse Sid Smith was Moore's sparring partner, along with another veteran of the ring, Sam Keller. Training went without a hitch and Moore was happy with his new surroundings. 'Stanmore is a peach of a place,' he told reporters. 'Before this fight with Jimmy, I never trained for more than seven days but I could stay here for a whole year and not worry.'[95]

In Tylorstown, meanwhile, Wilde had changed his regime slightly. Up until now, Jimmy had always sparred in the evenings, but while preparing to fight Joe Lynch he had found that he was

94 *Daily Mirror* 28 June 1919
95 *Daily Mirror* 4 July 1919

waking up stiff in the mornings. He told Benny Williams about it and they decided to change things around. From now on, sparring would be done in the early afternoon.

Ned Copp, Gomer Perkins and Young Colcombe pushed Wilde hard in sparring and, a few days before the fight, he was feeling confident and in top shape. Teddy Lewis, as always, was optimistically cautious. 'We have one great danger to guard against and that is over-confidence. This is going to be the fight of Jimmy's life. We have left nothing to chance. Outside the ring, Moore is a gentleman. In the ring he is a clever, cunning, crafty boxer.'[96]

The day before the fight, *Boxing* was confident of a Wilde victory as it previewed the fight. Moore, *Boxing* warned, had a tendency to slap with an open glove and telegraph his punches. Wilde could win the fight by throwing straight punches and by boxing scientifically. The editor also noted that Wilde fought best in the summer months when he was free from coughs and colds. With the fight taking place in July, the editor expected Wilde to win with a bit to spare.

As dawn broke on 17 July 1919, the hottest ticket in town was for the boxing at the Olympia in Kensington that evening. 'What a cosmopolitan assembly it was!' wrote *Sporting Life*. 'Every stratum of English life was represented from the royal family down to labourers.'[97]

As the great hall began to fill, the good omens seemed to be shining on the Welsh fighters. In the preliminary bouts, Jimmy's stablemate, Ned Copp from Treorchy, and Young Colcombe,

96 *Daily Mirror* 10 July 1919
97 *Sporting Life* 19 July 1919

a Tylorstown lad of immense promise, both won their fights on points.

At ten o'clock, a huge roar went up as Wilde climbed through the ropes. Above his corner was a huge Union Jack supported by poles. The next roar was for Pal Moore. Above his corner was the Stars and Stripes. As the two boxers were gloved up, another wave of excitement swept through the audience when the Prince of Wales and General Pershing, the Commander-in-Chief of the US forces, took their seats in the royal box.

During the introductions, conducted by master of ceremonies Harry Brevett, Wilde was a picture of concentration. Opposite him, Moore, a boxer so talented that world champions were unwilling to risk their titles against him, limbered up by swinging his arms and rotating his waist.

A hush of expectation descended on the great hall as the timekeeper, Mr Palmer, rang the bell for the first round. For one of the few times in his career, Wilde found himself in front of an opponent who carried his hands lower than he did. Both Moore's hands were down by his knees.

From the outset, as *Boxing* had predicted, Moore swung punches with an open glove. Wilde blocked most of them with his arms and shoulders, but the American was difficult to hit cleanly. Moore had a habit of retreating to the ropes where he would bend over double, his left arm and open glove fully extended, which kept Wilde from getting inside.

During the second and third rounds, Moore was extremely cautious. Perhaps, like Joe Lynch, it was the result of having so many 'no decision' bouts. Wilde won the rounds by doing all the forcing and throwing left-right combinations.

Throughout rounds four and five, Moore dashed around the ring like a dragonfly as Wilde relentlessly chased after him throwing punches. Wilde, however, was not reckless. As ever, every movement was economical. Not one punch was wasted. Every single feint had a purpose. Wilde was succeeding in making Moore miss and then scoring with effective counters.

By the sixth, Moore had started to realise the fight was getting away from him. He attacked more but was still slapping. The crowd implored the referee on more than half a dozen occasions to tell the American to close his gloves, but the third man in the ring, Eugene Corri, was unusually lenient and had no intention of penalising him.

From the seventh through to the end of the 11th, it was all Wilde. Moore's face was reddened by the left jabs and right hands he had taken. At the end of every round, he was drenched in water by his seconds while seated in his corner.

The 12th and 13th were even. Both Wilde and Moore, it seemed, needed to take a breather. Although the odd exchange was fast and furious, there was a lot of missing.

The 14th was the first round Moore won. For the first time in the fight, he closed his gloves and it had immediate results. A right connected, splitting Jimmy's lip.

In the 15th, Wilde drove Moore back as they exchanged fierce rallies. The American's cuffs were having little effect on Wilde, though, whereas Wilde's punches were taking their toll.

Moore needed a knockout to win. He was a mile behind as the bell clanged for round 16. Wilde sustained his second injury of the fight early in this round. Both men came together with their heads down. Moore's head happened to connect with Jimmy's first. Moore's head smashed into Wilde's face, tearing a piece of skin off his nose. Wilde reeled back in pain, shouting to Corri: 'That was his head!' Corri told them: 'Box on.'

Despite the injury to his nose, Wilde ploughed forward in the 17th. He shook Moore with a heavy right that sent him backwards on jittery legs, but the man from Memphis was proving to be a defensive genius, covering up and bobbing and weaving until the danger had passed.

The longer the fight went on, the stronger Wilde was getting. He pushed Moore to his limits in the 18th and 19th rounds with rapid left-right-left-right salvos. Moore was forced to clinch in search of respite.

In the 20th and final round, Wilde had victory in his sights. He was so excited that he lost his footing twice while tearing after Moore. Wilde was doing all the scoring. Moore, exhausted, came in to clinch, inadvertently shouldering Wilde in the face. Wilde took a step back, blinking. Realising that the referee was not going to warn Moore, Wilde got on his bicycle and kept out of punching distance until the bell. Corri, without a moment's hesitation, pointed to Wilde. Within seconds, the ring was invaded by well-wishers. Wilde, Moore and Corri were completely lost in the melee.

Wilde had completely dominated the fight. He had won 16 rounds, with Moore only managing to take two. The other two were even.

Moore told *Boxing*: 'I was hoping that from halfway my weight and extra strength would tell. Those swings of mine are the blows on which I count. They pass in America. I don't understand why they don't in this country, but I have no complaints against Mr Corri. I would like to meet Wilde again, but next time I will close my gloves. I have never come across better sportsmen in my life and I'm certain that if I did beat Wilde his warmest admirers would still have a few cheers for me.'

Wilde had every admiration for Moore. 'The collision in the 16th really stunned me. Moore apologised at once but it took the skin off my nose and the bleeding bothered me until the close. I was never in any doubt about the result. He is a real good fellow. A great, strong, game fighter who defends well and is not easy to land on. Those slaps hurt though, especially with the heel of the glove or the bony part of his wrist. If he punched correctly he would be a world beater. He seems to slam away and swing, trusting to luck. His seconds rubbed something greasy on him in the later rounds. It may have been liniment or something, but it got in my eyes and made them sting and water but I was always confident I had him beat.'[98]

98 *Boxing* 23 July 1919

18

A North American Adventure

WILDE SPENT what was left of the summer of 1919 playing golf and basking in the warm glow of contentment that his victories over Joe Lynch and Pal Moore, in particular, had given him.

Meanwhile, Teddy Lewis and David Hughes were busy arranging a six-month tour of America and Canada which would give the Americans a chance to see for themselves 'the Welsh Wonder'. If Jimmy could capture the public's imagination and perform as well as he had done in Britain, then the chances of making a fight with the world bantamweight champion Pete Herman would be significantly easier.

The plan was for Wilde to take part in ten 'no decision' bouts, the first being against the top bantamweight contender Jackie Sharkey in early December. After that, Wilde and Hughes – who was standing in for Teddy Lewis, who could not make the trip – would work closely with Charlie Harvey to make the other fights.

In early November, Jimmy, Elizabeth, Benny Williams and Hughes set sail from Liverpool aboard RMS *Baltic* for New York via Halifax, Nova Scotia.

For all four of them, it was a trip of a lifetime. They had all been looking forward to it with great anticipation for some time. The crossing, however, was rough and Elizabeth was the only person unaffected by seasickness.

As the *Baltic* made its way into New York, Jimmy described the skyline as 'a thing of wonder with its incredibly high buildings. It was like a fantasy. Majestic. Wonderful.' It was a breathtaking sight as Manhattan slowly came into view, and one that Jimmy, during his time working in the mines and fighting on the booths, could not have possibly imagined he would ever see.[99]

Fight agent Charlie Harvey greeted the quartet as they disembarked. To Wilde's surprise, a large crowd had gathered and they cheered him as he disembarked. After Wilde had signed a few autographs, Harvey whisked them off to the Imperial Hotel in New York City, where a lavish banquet awaited them. Wilde was grateful for the welcome, but the journey across the Atlantic had been an arduous one and he was mightily glad when the time came to retire to his hotel room.

Elizabeth had always cooked Jimmy's meals and she was determined to carry on doing so in New York. After a few days at the Imperial, she decided they should temporarily rent a flat so they would feel more at home instead of feeling like tourists in a bustling hotel.

Within a few days of settling in, Wilde received a cable from Otto Borcert, who, as well as being the owner of the Milwaukee

99 Jimmy Wilde *Fighting Was My Business* p.165

Brewers baseball team, was also a boxing promoter and joint owner of the Cream City Auditorium.

Wilde and Hughes were happy with the contract, the most important part of which stated that Sharkey must be no heavier than 8st 4lb at the weigh-in on the night of the fight. If Sharkey did come in over the weight, he would have to pay Wilde a $2,000 forfeit.

Sharkey was born in Italy in 1897. His parents had emigrated to New York City when he was still a toddler and he spent his youth as a street fighter and tearaway. Turning professional at just 16, Sharkey mainly fought in athletic clubs in New York and Pennsylvania.

'Little' Jackie, who stood 5ft 3in, was a bustling, all-action fighter who had fought all of the top men in the bantamweight division. In 1916 and 1917, he had taken part in 'no decision' bouts against Joe Lynch, Pal Moore, Johnny Coulon, Kid Williams and Joe Burman.

In August 1919, Sharkey had the two best performances of his career. He fought Pete Herman, the reigning world bantamweight champion, in Milwaukee and Detroit. Both fights went the full ten rounds and, although they were 'no decision' bouts, many of the newspaper reporters watching at ringside thought Sharkey had done enough to win on each occasion had a decision been announced.

With the contract signed, Jimmy, Elizabeth, Benny and David made the long train journey to snow-covered Milwaukee and Wilde set up camp in Wauwatosa, a small town six miles from the city.

The main difference Wilde found while training in the States was that boxers trained in public gyms where the man on the street could just walk in and watch the fighters train. This took him a little time to get used to, but the one thing Wilde could not get his head around was training in the same building as his opponent. He had quite a surprise when he was doing his workout on his first day at the gym and saw Sharkey being put through his paces on the other side of the room.

The night of 6 December 1919 was a bitterly cold one in Milwaukee. An estimated 7,500 people battled their way through a blizzard to see the legendary Welshman in action at the Cream City Auditorium.

Although Wilde and Sharkey fought at a fast pace, neither man did much damage to the other during the contest. Sharkey, uncharacteristically, fought a defensive fight and only came to life in the last 30 seconds of each round in an attempt to impress the ringside reporters.

Most of Sharkey's punches were blocked by Wilde's arms and shoulders, while Jimmy continually poked out jabs in an attempt to pierce Sharkey's watertight cross-armed guard. After ten soporific rounds, those at the *Milwaukee Sentinel,* somewhat predictably, thought Wilde had only won one round.

The following morning, Wilde woke up feeling depressed. He had arrived in America amid much fanfare, but the negative tone of the reports of his fight with Sharkey surprised and disappointed him.

Perhaps it was simply because Wilde had always been the subject of such glowing reports back home that he didn't know how to deal with negative press. A sense of proportion was needed. After all, he hadn't lost. The bout had been a 'no decision'. A week later, the man who had refereed the fight, Walter Houlihan, would write that, had a decision been announced, he would have given it to Wilde.

Wilde, feeling crestfallen in the immediate aftermath of the fight, returned to Wauwatosa. Luckily for him and Elizabeth, their old friend, Talbot O'Farrell, a music hall singer and comedian from Hull, regularly visited to entertain them.

With thick snow on the ground and sub-zero temperatures, Christmas was 'miserable and cold'. Jimmy, Elizabeth, Benny and David were 'afraid that the whole tour would flop'.[100]

Ironically, help came on Boxing Day in the form of the old lightweight contender Tommy Sullivan, who now worked as a matchmaker for the St Louis Athletic Club. He visited Jimmy at his apartment in Wauwatosa and offered him an eight-round 'no decision' bout against St Louis flyweight Johnny Asher in Asher's home town on 8 January. Wilde, who was desperate to get back in the ring and put the negative reports of the Sharkey fight behind him, agreed without hesitation.

Asher had done most of his boxing in the Army Expeditionary Force and was little more than a raw novice. When he climbed into the ring to fight Wilde, Asher had only been fighting professionally for nine months. Although he had faced Young Zulu Kid twice in 'no decision' bouts – and been voted the winner on both occasions by his local paper, the *St Louis Post* – not many in the fight game had paid much attention.

100 Jimmy Wilde *Fighting Was My Business* p.184

What became evident when the fight began was that what Asher lacked in skill, he more than made up for with bravery. Wilde put him down in the fourth, fifth and sixth and never stopped attacking. Asher was as game as they come and although he threw his fair share of punches, they lacked the necessary sting to force Wilde back. After eight one-sided rounds, the reporters from the *St Louis Post* had to concede that there was no way that they could say the local man had won. They all agreed that Wilde had won every round.

Wilde's dominant performance against Asher was the one he had been looking for. He returned to Milwaukee with a spring in his step and a feeling that the trip may be worthwhile after all.

By the time Jimmy and his team arrived back in Wauwatosa, Otto Borcert, who had read the reports of the Asher fight, had already arranged for Wilde to fight Mikey Ertle, the brother of bantamweight contender Johnny Ertle, at the end of January.

Wilde started the fight by scoring with left jabs which constantly unsettled Ertle, preventing him from landing any worthwhile punches of his own. In the second round, Wilde avoided most of Ertle's punches by shuffling out of range and then darted back in with fast left-right-left-right combinations.

With one minute gone in the third, Wilde rocked Ertle with a right that made the man from St Paul in Minnesota drop his hands. Sensing that Ertle was badly shaken, Wilde followed up with a straight left to the chin, which knocked Ertle to the canvas. Poor Mikey's senses were scrambled. He never moved as the referee counted him out.

Wilde and his camp were now full of confidence. The two conclusive performances against Asher and Ertle had quickly banished the anxieties which had plagued them during the festive period.

On 19 February 1920, Wilde took on Mickey Russell in his home town of Jersey City. The freezing cold weather and icy roads kept many away from the Armoury Hall on the night of the fight. The road conditions had been so bad that when Jimmy's cab got stuck in the snow, he had been tempted to get out and walk to the arena. Thankfully, the cab made it with plenty of time to spare.

The shouts of encouragement from Russell's supporters sounded eerily hollow in the huge, near-empty arena. Those who had braved the inclement weather saw a totally one-sided contest. Russell was beaten from pillar to post from the very outset. Russell was all but done when the bell rang to end the sixth and he was still badly dazed when he came out at the start of the seventh. A smashing right from Wilde finally broke Russell's resistance. With Russell hanging over the top rope, facing the sparse crowd in an helpless state, the referee jumped in and called off the fight.

News of Wilde's form seemed to have spread. His next four bouts on the tour all followed a similar pattern. Each opponent was intent on holding at every opportunity in an attempt to avoid being stopped. Patsy Wallace survived six rounds, Frankie Mason ran around the perimeter of the ring for 12 frustrating rounds and Young Zulu Kid, the man Wilde had faced in the first-ever world flyweight title fight in 1916, repeatedly ducked low whenever Wilde got near him in a stop-start ten-rounder.

Just nine days later, Wilde was in the ring again. This time he faced Alexander DeRenza, a heavy puncher from Philadelphia who fought under the name 'Battling' Al Murray.

Murray's reputation as a big hitter was proven in the first round. A thunderous left hook knocked Wilde to the canvas. Badly shaken, Wilde hung on to Murray for the remainder of the round.

For some reason known only to himself, Murray changed tactics at the start of the second. Instead of going after Wilde, who was still feeling the effects of the knockdown blow, Murray started boxing from long range. This played right into Wilde's hands. Murray had missed his big chance of scoring a massive upset. By the end of the second round, Wilde's head had cleared and he dominated the next five rounds. With Murray's face badly swollen, referee Billy Rocap stopped the fight in the eighth round.

The fight against Murray had been the most competitive by far since Wilde had arrived in America. So impressive was his showing, especially after he had to climb off the floor to win, that the sporting press firmly believed that, if Wilde were to meet Sharkey again, Sharkey would have little chance of lasting the distance, never mind winning.

This was music to Jimmy's ears as he and his small team spent a relaxing week at Freddie Welsh's health farm in Orangeburg in Upstate New York.

With fine spring weather in the offing, Wilde travelled next to Lawrence, Massachusetts for an open air fight against Bobby Dyson on 1 May.

Wilde had accepted $8,000 for the Dyson fight. However, when he weighed in, he and David Hughes noticed that there were motion picture cameras present. The filming of the fight, and the subsequent revenue that would be generated, had not been mentioned in Wilde's contract. Hughes promptly told the promoter that, unless they were paid a further $1,000, the fight was off. Fearing he would lose his top-of-the-bill attraction, the promoter offered Hughes and Wilde an extra $500, which they accepted.

Hughes had done well by holding out for more money. Poor Dyson was knocked out inside the first minute of the opening round in front of a huge crowd. The promoter was beside himself. The fight had not even lasted long enough to warrant it being sold to theatres.

'Battling' Al Murray deserved another chance at Wilde. A fortnight after Jimmy blew away Dyson, Wilde and Murray locked horns for a second time, this time at the National Athletic Club in Philadelphia.

Wilde had gone through the first fight in his mind many times. A couple of days before the return match, he told Elizabeth that he saw himself stopping Murray early, especially if Murray charged in recklessly like he had in the first round of their previous encounter. Elizabeth agreed.

Charging out is exactly what Murray did in Philadelphia. The sheer volume of punches forced Wilde to back up. Murray's

'Sunday punch', his left hook, again shook Wilde, only this time it wasn't heavy enough to put him over. Just before the bell, Wilde rocked Murray with a right that hit him square on the jaw.

In their first fight, Murray had gone on the defensive after hurting Wilde. Now he himself had been hurt but Murray went on the offensive. However, the thudding right he had taken near the end of the first round had taken the edge off his punches. Realising this more acutely than anyone else, Wilde decided to mix it in the centre of the ring with the hometown favourite.

When Murray left himself open midway through the second, Wilde pounced. A terrific left hook put Murray face down on the mat. Murray bravely rose on unsteady legs after taking an eight count, but the fight was over. Swaying left and right, his eyes glazed, Murray was helped back to his corner by the referee, Pat O'Brien. For Jimmy, the fight had gone exactly the way he told Elizabeth it would.

Wilde's last fight of the tour was a return match over ten rounds with the ultra-defensive Patsy Wallace in Toronto on 24 May. Wallace, whose real name was Pasquale Appalucci, had been born in Italy. His parents, who emigrated in search of work when he was still a young boy, settled in Philadelphia. Appalucci, like so many Italian immigrants, adopted a ring name at the start of his career. Within three years, he had fought 'no decision' bouts against some quality fighters including 'Battling' Al Murray, Young Montreal, Frankie Mason, Pete Herman, Jackie Sharkey and Johnny Buff.

Early in the second round, Wallace managed to cut Wilde's lip with a cuffing punch. It bled profusely and Wilde's mouth, chin and chest were crimson as he pressed forward trying to breach Wallace's defence.

In between rounds, Benny Williams managed to stop the bleeding. Wallace attacked more from the third round onwards, targeting Wilde's injured mouth. The injury looked worse than it was, but it started to bleed heavily again without pressure being applied to it and Wilde, through clever defensive work and Wallace's inability to connect with any sort of worthwhile punch, succeeded in protecting the injury for the remainder of the bout.

As the bell went at the end of the tenth, Wallace's furious cornermen raced into the ring to confront the referee, Lou Marsh, who had constantly warned their fighter to stop holding throughout the fight. The local police had to act quickly and usher the ref to safety.

Jimmy's tour of North America was now over. He, Elizabeth, Benny and David were looking forward to getting back to Wales. For Jimmy and Elizabeth, visiting so many different cities in America and Canada had been the real highlight of the trip. Not the boxing. They found Philadelphia as awesome as New York City, the people of Toledo, Ohio, were as hospitable as any Jimmy and Elizabeth had ever met and the journey along the St Lawrence River to Ontario had been breathtakingly beautiful.

The trip, after an unpromising start, had been enjoyable, as well as financially rewarding. It was estimated that Wilde earned in excess of $30,000 (worth almost £400,000 in 2024) from his 11 fights. 'It was a remarkable time. Full of light and shadow. One moment feeling on top of the world, the next in the deepest gloom.' All told, Wilde's time in America and Canada had been 'tremendously exhilarating'.[101]

101 Jimmy Wilde *Fighting Was My Business* p.222

19

The Tiger Of New Orleans

WHEN HE returned to England in the summer of 1920, Wilde already had one eye on retirement. He told Teddy Lewis that there were only two fights that interested him - a meeting with the great Pete Herman or a match against Jackie Sharkey.

Wilde was now 28, an advanced age for a little man in the fight game, and, while he had once relished the prospect of training and sparring every day, he now preferred to be out on the golf course or playing a few frames of snooker, which was his other great passion.

Along with nine-year-old David and four-year-old Verdun, Jimmy and Elizabeth had plenty to keep them both busy. With the money Jimmy had earned from the American tour, the Wildes decided to purchase a new house in Radyr, a short distance from Cardiff.

Elizabeth was relieved that Jimmy's boxing career was slowing down. Although boxing had been good to them and had provided them with a life that they could only have dreamt of when they first met, the constant training and fighting had brought its pressures. Teddy Lewis agreed with Wilde that, at this stage in his career, it was pointless travelling the length and breadth of the country every week fighting young up-and-comers, who had no chance of winning, for relatively small purses.

C.B. Cochran, the Brighton-born theatre manager who had branched out into boxing promoting, had been having serious talks with Herman's promoter, Rube Welch, throughout August. Cochran wanted to bring Herman over to London to fight Wilde at the Holborn Stadium at the end of September. Not only would it be a great fight, it would also give Wilde the chance to become a two-weight world champion.

Cochran contacted Teddy Lewis about the prospect of Wilde taking the fight. Teddy, with a spring in his step, immediately went round to Jimmy's to tell him of the ongoing negotiations between Cochran and Welch. To Teddy's surprise, Wilde was unenthusiastic. He was enjoying his time away from the rigours and strains of the ring. Teddy resorted to pleading. This was the *one* big fight left for him. A chance to win the world bantamweight title. Not to mention a £5,000 (worth around £180,000 in 2024) payday.

Jimmy looked at Elizabeth. They both went quiet. Wilde looked at Teddy. A purse of that size and the chance of boxing immortality were extremely tempting. Wilde quietly sat there, weighing up the options. He knew he could whip himself into top shape if he was focused enough. Jimmy told Teddy he would take the fight. Teddy was ecstatic. He went back and told Cochran. The fight was on for 27 September.

With the date set, Wilde started light training. On the other side of the Atlantic, Herman was taking part in 'no decision' bouts. He was having serious problems getting down to 8st 6lb. By mid-September, Cochran was getting anxious. With the fight only a couple of weeks away, Herman had not yet arrived in England. Welch sent Cochran a cable saying Herman could not make the weight. The fight was off.

Cochran, who had lost a significant amount of cash, was beside himself. He promptly told the press he was 'finished with boxing' and that he had made his decision with a 'great deal of regret'. The incensed Cochran kept his word and never promoted another boxing show.[102]

With the fight off, Wilde settled back into the routine he had enjoyed for the best part of the summer. He felt sorry for Cochran, who he classed as a friend, but was ambivalent about fighting Herman. Wilde had a strong feeling that the fight would never happen. *Boxing* firmly believed that Herman was afraid to risk his title against Wilde, irrespective of where the fight was held.

Rube Welch, however, was still hopeful the fight could be made. With Cochran now out of the picture, Welch contacted London-based promoter Leon Pollock, who also had close ties with the International Sporting Club of New York. In the second week of November, Welch and Pollock signed articles for Herman to fight Wilde at White City Stadium in London (the venue was later changed to the Royal Albert Hall) on 13 January 1921.

102 *Daily Mirror* 18 September 1920

Wilde's purse was reported to be £8,000, with Herman getting £7,000 plus training expenses.

Welch was so concerned that Herman would back out of the fight at the last minute again that he made Herman pay the New York State Athletic Commission a $2,000 guarantee that he would fulfil his contract to fight Wilde on the agreed date. If Herman broke the contract, he would not only have to pay the forfeit, but he would also be barred from fighting in New York on his return. This also meant Herman would be at the commission's mercy as to when they might see fit to lift the ban.

Nine days before Herman was due to sail to England, Joe Lynch knocked out Jackie Sharkey in the 15th round at Madison Square Garden in New York to further solidify his status alongside Pal Moore as a top contender for Herman's title. No one in the Garden that night could have foreseen Herman fighting Lynch in between fighting Wilde. But that is exactly what happened.

Instead of leaving New York on 11 December, Herman stayed in Manhattan and fought Lynch on 22 December at Madison Square Garden. For the first time since November 1917 (when Herman had last defended his title against Frankie Burns) Herman entered the ring 1½lb inside the bantamweight limit. With Lynch weighing 8st 5lb, Herman was risking his title for the first time in three years.

Lynch kept Herman on the end of his left jab for the entire 15 rounds. Herman was listless and cautious throughout and did little attacking. He may well have been weight-drained. Lynch, who won the fight handily, was the new world bantamweight champion.

Ever since the decision was announced that night at the Garden, there have been rumours that Herman lost the fight on purpose so that the title stayed in America. Who came up with this story is unknown, but it has been repeated in many history books by many different writers. Would a great, proud fighter like Herman 'lend' his title to a fellow American simply to keep it in the country?

Herman, who was already losing the sight in one eye when he fought Lynch, spoke about the fight to author Peter Heller 50 years later. 'It was a very smoky night that night. The smoke was like fog in the arena. Lynch would be in his corner and I would be in mine and I couldn't see Lynch. Lynch beat me but I think the smoke affected me that night. I couldn't see him. At no time was I hurt.'

The next part of the interview is a revealing insight into how much the title meant to Herman. 'You're the champion of the world. You lose that and you lose what you've been fighting for for a long time. You feel bad about it 'cos it's somethin' you wanna keep.'[103]

Whether Herman was told to lose the title can never be proven. What was certain was that he would be coming to England to fight Wilde without the world bantamweight title.[104]

Pete Herman was born Peter Gulotta on 12 February 1896 in Convent, Louisiana. He became interested in boxing while working as a shoeshine boy at a local barbershop where he would

103 *In This Corner...! Forty World Champions Tell Their Stories* Peter Heller p.51

104 Seven months after losing the title, Herman regained it when he won a 15-round decision over Lynch at Ebbets Field, Brooklyn.

read about fights in the *Police Gazette*. By the time Herman was 16, he was fighting professionally in local sporting clubs.

An effective body puncher, Herman fought 'no decision' bouts against the best men of his era on multiple occasions. He fought Johnny Rosner twice, had three bouts with Jabez White, four with Young Zulu Kid, two against Pal Moore, five with Jackie Sharkey and three with Joe Lynch.

In June 1914, Herman fought the world bantamweight champion Kid Williams in a 'no decision' bout. Herman acquitted himself so well that they fought again five days before Herman's 20th birthday, this time with Williams's title on the line. Herman gave Williams all kinds of trouble and, although the referee, Billy Rocap, declared the fight a draw, many of those at ringside thought Herman had done enough to win.

Herman's manager, Sam Goldman, knew his boy had the beating of Kid Williams. He put up $5,000 to persuade the champ to risk his title in a return and gave Williams the luxury of choosing his own referee as an extra incentive to accept the fight. Williams chose Billy Rocap.

On 9 January 1917, at the Louisiana Auditorium, Herman got his second opportunity to win the title. Herman left nothing to chance. Fighting like a human buzzsaw, he floored Williams in the fifth and again in the 12th. After 20 rounds of hard fighting, Rocap awarded Herman the decision by nine rounds to eight, with three even.

After successfully defending his title against Frankie Burns in November 1917, Herman took part in 46 'no decision' bouts against all of the top bantamweights before losing his title to Lynch just before Christmas 1920.

Herman arrived at Southampton on New Year's Day 1921. Alongside him was the heavyweight contender Battling Levinsky, who was due to fight Bombardier Billy Wells on the same show. After disembarking, Herman and Levinsky were taken to their training quarters at Thames Ditton in Surrey.

When reporters went to watch Herman in training, it soon became obvious to them that he was not going to give much away. He seemed to hang back in sparring and they came away having learned very little.

Back in Radyr, Wilde was disappointed that Herman had lost his world title to Lynch. When Jimmy had signed the contract, it had clearly stated that Herman's world title would be at stake. Wilde never expected Herman to risk his title against someone of Lynch's calibre in between fighting him, let alone lose it. Teddy Lewis would have been well within his rights to pull Wilde out of the fight.

Nevertheless, Wilde was pragmatic. Title or no title, Herman was still the best bantamweight in the world. Wilde was under no illusions; this would be the toughest fight of his career. If he did beat Herman, it would easily rank as his greatest ever win, especially after a seven-month lay-off.

Although he was confident of winning, Wilde had misgivings about the fight. He and Teddy had wanted a 15-round bout, but the Americans had insisted on it being a 20-rounder. Wilde knew that, at the age of 28, 20 rounds was going to be hard going against a man of Herman's ability.

Wilde's other major concern was whether Herman would stick to the clause in the contract stating he should weigh 8st 6lb or under at the ringside weigh-in shortly before the first bell. Fighting Herman at that weight was going to be hard enough. If the American came into the ring three or four pounds heavier than the agreed weight, then Wilde knew his task would be virtually impossible.

Throughout his career, Wilde had never been ruffled by any situation outside of the ring. Having to work on rowdy booths and in hostile working men's clubs had instilled in him a cast iron temperament. The fight against Herman, however, was different. From the moment Teddy Lewis signed the contract, Wilde had the feeling something wasn't quite right. First of all, there had been the postponement in September. Then, when the fight had been rescheduled, the Americans had got their way by having the fight over 20 rounds when Wilde had wanted 15 and, to cap it all, Herman's world title would not be on the line.

Those feelings of unease had not gone away when Wilde arrived at the Royal Albert Hall on the night of the fight. For the first time in his illustrious career, apart from when he had unwisely fought Tancy Lee while unwell, Wilde did not feel as if he was going to win.

Things were about to get worse. While the final preliminary fight was in progress, Wilde reminded Lewis that it would soon be time for Herman to go to the ringside weigh-in. Lewis went over to Herman's dressing room. Sam Goldman told him that

Herman had weighed in at two o'clock that afternoon. Lewis reminded Goldman that they had agreed to weigh in at ringside 15 minutes before the first bell. Goldman showed Lewis the contract, which stated that Herman was to weigh in at 2pm. Lewis and Goldman's signatures were both at the bottom of the contract. Goldman told Lewis in no uncertain terms that Herman would not be going to the scales again.

Teddy Lewis was now in a panic. He had made a big mistake by not going through the contract with a fine-tooth comb. Both he and Wilde knew Herman was probably 8st 10lb or even heavier after having eight hours since weighing in that afternoon.

Things were not going well out in the hall either. Battling Levinsky had pulled out of his fight with Bombardier Billy Wells with a damaged elbow just minutes before they were due in the ring and those who were seated in the upper gallery were unable to see the ring because it was obscured by a canopy that was covering the ring lights.

With the arguments over the weigh-in causing a further delay, the crowd were growing impatient. Teddy wanted Wilde to pull out of the fight. 'I do not remember being on edge as much as I was that evening,' Jimmy would remember. 'I knew that the Prince of Wales was waiting, with Lord Lonsdale and many other prominent folk. I hated the idea of letting them down. The whole trouble had come about because Teddy had not scrutinised Herman's agreement to make sure that it was identical with mine.'[105]

105 Jimmy Wilde *Fighting Was My Business* p.230

Teddy felt terrible about the situation. Wilde tried to reassure him that it was just one of those things. Fearing that Wilde would pull out of the fight, Lord Lonsdale and the Prince of Wales went to see him in his dressing room.

'Do you think you can beat him, Jimmy?' the prince asked.

Wilde shook his head.

'I'll do my best Your Highness, but I don't think much of my chances after all this bother. He will have to knock me senseless to win, though.'[106]

With that, the prince and Lord Lonsdale wished Jimmy luck and made their way back to the royal box.

As both boxers sparred for an opening in the first round, it soon became apparent to those watching that Wilde had no zip or go in him. He seemed to be totally devoid of his usual energy and there was no spring in his movements.

Early in the first round, Herman measured Wilde by holding out his left arm and then threw a rapid right that struck Wilde square on the chin. There was a gasp around the hall as the punch landed. Herman would never have been able to do that to the version of Jimmy Wilde who had gone to America. What was even more worrying was the fact that Herman would successfully repeat the move five more times during the next few rounds.

Boxing wrote that, just two minutes into the fight, Wilde appeared 'no longer the fighter he had been' and that they had not thought much of his chances. 'In all boxing history, we have never seen a falling off so complete and so rapid.'[107]

106 Ibid p.231
107 *Boxing* 19 January 1921

Things got worse for Wilde in the second. Herman hit him with a thudding right that visibly wobbled him. Many years later, Wilde would often wonder whether Herman had realised how close he had been to finishing the fight there and then.

In the third round, Wilde seemed to have recovered and he attacked Herman for the first time in the fight with a left-right combination, but he was still uncharacteristically lethargic and his punches lacked any sort of snap. Herman, a renowned body puncher, stopped Wilde in his tracks with crippling body shots. Wilde was the busier, but Herman's punches carried the greater power.

Herman was warned by the referee for an unintentional low blow in the fourth. Low blows are an occupational hazard against a body puncher and Herman was concentrating solely on Wilde's sides and mid-section, landing hard, hurtful, strength-sapping blows.

Those watching at the Albert Hall knew that this was not the same Wilde who had beaten Joe Lynch and Pal Moore. Wilde, it seemed, had grown old overnight. He was fighting as if he knew he couldn't win and seemed devoid of confidence.

Wilde finally got his left jab working in the sixth but, whereas it had once been a waspish, stinging punch, it was now nothing more than an irritation to Herman, who slipped or parried it away before unleashing lefts and rights of his own to Wilde's battered ribcage.

Herman upped the pace in the seventh, driving Wilde back to the ropes. The American rained lefts and rights on Wilde and many in the crowd feared that the referee may step in and stop the fight, but Jimmy gritted his teeth and forced Herman back with a two-fisted barrage.

Herman fought in close during the eighth and ninth. His greater strength was starting to tell and the body punches were weakening Wilde at a rapid rate.

The power of Herman's punches was sharply brought into focus in the ninth. Wilde attempted to block the American's left with the palm of his right glove. The force of Herman's blow knocked Wilde's own glove back against his face. A heavy right to the side of the head had Wilde badly shaken near the end of the round and there was a sigh of relief all around the hall when the bell rang.

Wilde was looking weary at the start of the 11th. As Herman attacked incessantly, Wilde bobbed, weaved and ducked for all he was worth.

The 12th and 13th proved to be Jimmy's best rounds of the fight. He found some energy from somewhere and hurt Herman with a straight left and a follow-up right hand over the top. For the first time in the fight, Wilde was slipping most of Herman's punches rather than standing there and taking them.

In the 14th, Wilde began beating Herman to the punch, which forced the man from New Orleans to hold on. The crowd was willing Jimmy on but his superior volume of punches was instantly negated by the extra weight of Herman's.

Wilde put some fast left-right-left-right combinations together in the 15th. Herman's defence, however, was superb. Few of Wilde's punches got through and, near the end of the round,

Herman badly hurt him with yet another hard right to the jaw that made Wilde's legs buckle.

Wilde came out for the 16th round looking totally spent. It was becoming obvious to those in the hall that Wilde was not going to last another five rounds. He had not thrown a right hand of any significance since very early in the fight (after the fight, Wilde told reporters he had damaged it) and he had to use all his defensive nous, which in itself was very tiring, as Herman bombarded him with punches throughout the round. Hard rights repeatedly bounced off Wilde's jaw. He showed tremendous punch resistance and heart to make it to the bell.

The amount of punishment Wilde had absorbed in the 16th round forced him to instantly go on the defensive at the start of the 17th. Herman, sensing that Wilde was all in, forced him to the ropes. Two left jabs and a right to Wilde's jaw sent him tumbling through the ropes, the back of his head hitting the ring canopy with a sickening thud. Wilde, who no longer knew where he was, was now surviving on instinct alone. Somehow he managed to climb back into the ring by the count of seven. Herman met him with a left and two smashing rights that put Wilde down. He got up at seven. Half bent over, Wilde was unable to move his legs. Herman hammered him with lefts and rights until he went down for a third time. As referee Jack Smith counted, Wilde bravely got to his feet. Smith had seen enough. He grabbed Wilde around his waist to prevent him falling over and 'carried the little hero to his corner'.[108]

---

108 *Boxing* 19 January 1921

20

Pancho

WILDE HAD taken a bad beating from Herman. He had been severely concussed after the first knockdown in the 17th round and, for several weeks afterwards, he complained of having a constant headache.

Although the fight with Herman had been financially rewarding for him, it had not been good for his health. Many years later, he would often comment on how it would have been better for him in the long run if he had been knocked out in the second round; that way he would not have taken the many punches he did throughout the next 15 rounds.

Even though Wilde knew that taking that amount of punishment had not done him any good, he was still a fighter through and through. Later on in his life, he told reporters he had no regrets about fighting Herman and that, if he could go back in time, he would fight him again. The only thing he would have changed was all the nonsense beforehand about the contracts and the weigh-in.

While he was recuperating at home, the sporting press was

busy speculating as to who Wilde would fight next. Jim Higgins, the British bantamweight champion from Hamilton in Scotland, was the favourite, along with the top Frenchman Charles Ledoux.

Neither fight interested Wilde, though. He had been boxing for the best part of 14 years and was looking forward to a life away from the ring. Although he had not officially announced it, Wilde was, to all intents and purposes, retired.

For the first time in his life, Jimmy could get up in the morning and not have to face the prospect of training for a fight. Now aged 29, it seemed his metabolism was slowing down at last. Without the rigours of training every day, he quite naturally put on a few pounds. Even so, he was still only 7½st. A daily round of golf and chasing after young Verdun were now his most strenuous workouts.

In 1923, after two years out of the ring, Wilde was still classed as the British and world flyweight champion, even though he had not fought anyone at that weight for four years.

Quite why the NSC had not declared the British title as being vacant so that the division could get moving again was something of a mystery. It would have been better for all concerned had the NSC nominated two challengers to fight for the vacant crown. There were several good domestic fighters, such as Plymouth's Frankie Ash and Salford's Jack Kid Doyle, who could have fought each other to fill the void and lift the division out of its slumber.

Likewise with Wilde's world title. After winning it, Wilde had never defended it due to the lack of suitable contenders around at that time. Four year later, however, the flyweights were gaining in popularity at a rapid rate in America, mainly due to the skilful but light-hitting New Yorker Frankie Genaro and the whirlwind from the Philippines, Pancho Villa.

Genaro was born on 26 August 1901 in New York City. Standing at just 5ft 2in, his childhood dream was to be a jockey, but he grew tired of cleaning out stables while waiting for a chance to ride and so turned his attention to boxing instead. Genaro was a natural. Just one year after having his first amateur fight, Genaro won a gold medal in the flyweight division at the 1920 Olympics in Antwerp when he outpointed Anders Pederson of Denmark.

Later that autumn, Genaro turned professional, stopping Joe Colletti in the second round in New York. Genaro was so talented that, in just his tenth professional bout, he took on the vastly more experienced Johnny Rosner in New York and clearly outpointed him after ten rounds of masterful boxing. In 1922, Genaro cemented his claim as America's top flyweight when he twice outpointed the aggressive, hard-hitting Charley Phil Rosenberg (who would go on to win the world bantamweight title in 1925) and outboxed Pancho Villa, a fighter who was being touted as a future world flyweight champion.

Pancho Villa was born Francisco Guilledo on the island of Negros in the Philippines on 1 August 1901. Both his parents worked for a wealthy landowner but, when Francisco was just six months old, his father abandoned his family and joined the US Navy.

Young Francisco grew up in abject poverty. To support his mother, who raised goats to earn a living, he spent his childhood cutting sugar canes, shining shoes and doing any other odd jobs that would bring in money.

When he was just 11, Francisco and a friend stowed away and made their way to Iloilo City on Panay Island and did anything they could to earn a few pesos. The two boys soon decided to move on again. They hid on a ship and headed north to Manila, where they settled in the Tondo district, the capital city's most destitute area.

One day, while he was hustling in the street, Francisco got talking to a local boxer, Elino Flores. He persuaded Francisco to go along to the gym and, within a few weeks, he was earning small amounts of money from sparring with the other fighters. One session, in particular, was about to change Francisco's life forever.

The 16-year-old, who weighed no more than 6st, was sparring one afternoon with Flores, who was a fully fledged featherweight. Out of nowhere, Francisco floored Flores with a perfectly timed right cross. Flores's trainer, Pacquito Villa, who had been watching the little youngster for some weeks, now knew he had a potential champion on his hands.

Pacquito Villa wasted little time after seeing Francisco drop Flores. Knowing that the young man was living on the streets, Pacquito took in Francisco and, within weeks, he had legally adopted him. Francisco Guilledo became Pancho Villa.

Pacquito had worked in boxing gyms in Manila all his life. His job as a trainer served a dual purpose. He was also a talent scout for Frank Churchill, the most influential boxing manager in the Philippines. Churchill, an American-born circus and racetrack owner, had close ties with all the top American fight promoters, most notably Tex Rickard.

Born in Kansas City in 1870, Rickard moved to Henrietta, Texas, after the death of his father and worked there as a horse wrangler. He was elected marshal of Henrietta in 1913, but moved to Alaska two years later after the death of his wife and three-month-old son.

It was in Alaska that Rickard heard of the Klondike gold rush. He panned for gold ore and sold his holdings for $60,000, heading to Yukon in Canada, where he opened a saloon. An inveterate gambler, every cent Rickard earned, he lost at the poker table or roulette wheel.

With less than $40 in his pocket, Rickard headed to Goldfield, Nevada, where there was another gold rush in progress and, by 1906, he was running the Northern Saloon and Casino. It was in this dirt-rich town that Rickard promoted his first boxing match, the foul-filled world lightweight championship fight between Joe Gans and Battling Nelson. With gate receipts of more than $69,000, Rickard was up and running. Many more huge promotions followed. Johnson-Jeffries in 1910, Willard-Dempsey in 1919 and Dempsey-Carpentier in 1921, a fight which produced boxing's first million-dollar gate and made Rickard known all over the world as boxing's greatest promoter.

Villa made his debut in 1919 and, within three years under Churchill's careful guidance, had compiled a 48-2-3 record. With no one left for Villa to fight in the Philippines, Churchill contacted Rickard in New York. When Churchill told Rickard he had a fighter who was a flyweight version of Jack Dempsey, Rickard knew he would go down well with the New York fight crowd. In May 1922, Villa, Churchill and Pacquito set sail for America to make their fortune.

Although he had swept all before him in his native country, Villa soon found that boxing in America was a different proposition to boxing in Manila.

His first fight on American soil was a 12-round 'no decision' bout against Abe Goldstein in New Jersey on 7 June 1922. Goldstein neutralised Villa's attacks by keeping him off balance with a ramrod left jab. The ringside reporters were unanimous that Goldstein had won comfortably.

One month later, Villa fought Genaro and was comprehensively outboxed for 12 rounds by the slick New Yorker. Fortunately for Villa, it was a 'no decision' bout.

It had been an inauspicious start for Villa. Churchill and Rickard knew they had to get him back on the winning trail fast. Putting him in with Goldstein and Genaro had, in hindsight, been over-ambitious. Villa won his next four fights against less accomplished men and was matched against Genaro again on 22 August 1922.

Genaro, as he had done in their first meeting, boxed brilliantly to win on points after ten rounds. Losing to Genaro, however, had not damaged Pancho's reputation too much. His all-action style of fighting was proving to be immensely popular with the fans. Although Genaro was a superb boxer, the people of New

York had proven with their hard-earned cash that they would rather watch Pancho.

Tex Rickard realised this more than anybody. He appreciated Genaro's skill, but he knew that Villa's come-forward, attacking style drew larger crowds. Genaro had more than earned his chance to challenge Johnny Buff for the American flyweight title, but Rickard knew he could sell more tickets, and make more money, by putting Villa in the ring with Buff.

On 14 September 1922, more than 12,000 people turned out to watch Villa take the American title from Buff in the 11th round at Ebbets Field in Brooklyn. Two months later, 15,000 saw Villa make his debut at Madison Square Garden, where he retained his title by beating Abe Goldstein by decision. After Villa had outpointed Terry Martin in December, it was impossible for Rickard to ignore Frankie Genaro any longer. Their third meeting was arranged for 1 March 1923.

Towards the end of February 1923, Tom O'Rourke, the matchmaker for the New York Polo Grounds, sent a telegram to Teddy Lewis offering Wilde the chance to defend his world title against the winner of the upcoming fight between Genaro and Villa. Wilde, O'Rourke said, would receive 37.5 per cent of the gate receipts. Teddy promptly told O'Rourke that Wilde was now retired.

This was not what O'Rourke or Rickard, in particular, wanted to hear. Rickard cabled Wilde directly. It was the first Wilde had heard of it. Teddy had not mentioned anything about a fight with either Genaro or Villa to him. Wilde went round to Teddy's.

'What does this mean, look you?' Jimmy asked, showing Teddy the letter.

'You've told me nothing about this.'

'I didn't intend to,' Teddy replied. 'You're retired, Jimmy. That's all there is to it.'[109]

As far as Teddy was concerned, that was the end of the matter. Wilde, though, was tempted by the offer. Despite the fact he had not fought for two years, he was still confident he could beat any flyweight in the world, especially a light puncher like Genaro, who was heavily favoured to outpoint Villa again. After all, Wilde reasoned, he had only ever lost once to a flyweight and that had been when he was weakened by the flu.

Jimmy went home and told Elizabeth. Surprisingly, she was in favour of him taking the fight. They invited Teddy round to talk it through. Teddy thought it was a bad idea. At 31, Wilde was ancient for a flyweight and he had not trained for two years. Teddy put his case forward, but he knew Jimmy well enough to know he had already made up his mind. Reluctantly, Teddy sent Rickard and O'Rourke a telegram telling them Wilde had agreed terms.

One week later, Genaro and Villa faced each other for a third time in front of 13,000 spectators at Madison Square Garden. Once again, it was a bull versus matador encounter, with Genaro boxing on the back foot while Villa constantly came forward looking to land one big pay-off punch. The fight was a lot closer than the previous two but, after 15 rounds, Genaro

109 Jimmy Wilde *Fighting Was My Business* p.237

was announced the winner and the new American flyweight champion by a split decision.

Rickard, O'Rourke and Genaro's manager, Phil Bernstein, met the following day to discuss terms for the fight with Wilde. Bernstein, however, did not like the terms Rickard was offering and refused to accept them.

It is likely that Rickard offered Bernstein unreasonable terms knowing he would turn them down. Villa was a far bigger draw at the box office than Genaro and would generate more money. The fact Genaro was the best flyweight in America and more deserving of a chance at the title did not matter. Such facts count for nothing in boxing when big money is involved.

Rickard immediately got in touch with Frank Churchill who, predictably, accepted the fight against Wilde without hesitation. The fight was made for 16 June at the Polo Grounds in New York.

Wilde arrived in New York aboard RMS *Aquitania* on 18 May 1923. Six days earlier at Southampton, he had told a group of reporters who were there to wave him off and wish him luck that he felt 'fit and confident' and it would be 'unwise to back the other fellow'.[110]

When Wilde disembarked, the first thing he noticed was the oppressive heat. Most days, it was 32 degrees Celsius or above. The hot weather, however, did not deter him from spending most of his time playing golf with American sportswriters and eating copious amounts of ice cream to keep cool.

---

110 *The Sportsman* 12 May 1923

While Jimmy was based in Jersey City, Villa was keeping in shape at Pompton Lakes. Large crowds gathered daily to watch him spar and hit the heavy bag. The American fight crowd could not get enough of the man who the sports papers called 'the Miniature Dempsey'. At the end of each training session, Pancho would entertain the crowd by singing a song while playing his ukulele.

Heavy rain on 16 June forced the fight to be put back two days. On the afternoon of Monday 18 June, Wilde and Villa weighed in at 'Philadelphia' Jack O'Brien's gym in Manhattan. Both fighters looked pensive as they were called to the scales. Wilde, wearing only a white towel around his waist, weighed in at 7st 11½lb, the heaviest of his career. His pale skin, which had once been taut, now looked soft and podgy. Villa (7st 12lb), on the other hand, was honed to perfection. His swarthy complexion seemed to accentuate the tightness of his muscles, which bulged from his tiny frame.

Just before 10pm, ring announcer Joe Humphreys introduced Wilde and Villa to the 23,000 spectators who had paid $96,000 to be at New York's Polo Grounds. During the next 21 minutes, they would witness possibly the greatest fight that has ever taken place in the flyweight division.

Humphreys called both men to the centre of the ring, where Wilde, Villa and referee Patsy Haley posed for the newspaper photographers. Haley then quickly gave his final instructions to both men before they returned to their respective corners to await the opening bell.

Wilde was the first to land with two sharp left jabs that thudded into Villa's face. As Wilde went to throw another jab, Villa bent his knees slightly and caught the punch on his crossed arms. Wilde forced Villa to the ropes with a left-right-left-right-left-right salvo. Villa came back with a heavy right hook which connected with Wilde's jaw and rocked him to his heels. Wilde retreated to the middle of the ring, knocking Villa's head back with three hard left jabs before stunning Pancho with two hard rights. As Villa backed away, Wilde scored again with a rapid left-right-left-right combination. Villa stung Wilde with a left hook and a cuffing right which landed on Wilde's left ear, causing him to momentarily touch the canvas with his gloves. Referee Haley shouted 'No knockdown,' wiped Jimmy's gloves on his white shirt and told both men to resume fighting. Villa came on strong in the last 30 seconds of the round, scoring with vicious left hooks that knocked Wilde's head sideways. A left-right forced Wilde back at the bell, but he had won the opening round.

Pancho kept coming forward in the second. Wilde scored with two lefts followed by a right. Villa rocked Wilde with a left hook. Wilde looked sharp, but Villa was physically the stronger man when the two worked in close. Wilde drove Villa to the ropes with a four-punch combination. Villa retaliated with lefts and rights to Wilde's head and body. Two left hooks in succession staggered Wilde, who reeled backwards across the ring. It seemed that only the ropes kept him up. Wilde dug deep and threw lefts and rights to Villa's head. Wilde was throwing more punches, but Pancho's heavy left hook was rocking Wilde time and again.

Wilde complained to Haley after Villa had landed with a left hook and then brought the punch back across, hitting Wilde again with the back of his glove.

No one in the Polo Grounds that steamy night could ever have envisaged what would happen next. As the bell clanged to end the second round, Wilde turned away from Villa and naturally lowered his arms as he walked towards his corner. Villa followed him and threw a right swing at Wilde's jaw that he never saw coming. Wilde collapsed on to his side. Some in the crowd shouted 'Foul!' Wilde's cornermen, who were already in the ring, picked him up and propped him on his stool. Wilde was half unconscious. It had clearly been a foul blow after the bell. There is no doubt that Wilde should have been awarded the fight on a foul, which was the rule at that time. Nowadays, the fight would have been called off and recorded as a 'no contest'.

Haley, however, took no action. He explained to reporters after the fight that he had turned away from the fighters on hearing the bell and had not seen the foul blow land. Benny Williams worked feverishly on Wilde in the corner and somehow managed to bring him round and push him out for the third round.

Out on his feet, with a cut under his right eye, Wilde took everything Pancho could throw at him, so much so that the Filipino was on the verge of punching himself out. Two minutes into the round, Wilde seemed to have recovered some of his equilibrium, landing lefts and rights to Villa's head and body. *Boxing* reported that 'had this been the Jimmy Wilde we used to know, the fight would have ended there. But we were watching the ghost of a great champion who was trying vainly to turn back the drift of the years.'[111]

In the fourth and fifth, Wilde continued to land left jabs that Villa took flush in the face. Villa continued to walk forward with his arms crossed over his face while Wilde fired in lefts and rights. Both fighters engaged in fierce exchanges on the ropes. Ominously, Villa's left hook shook Jimmy off balance every time it landed.

The sixth round was equally as torrid as the five which preceded it. Wilde and Villa stood toe to toe, flailing away at each other. Villa was warned by the referee for 'back handing' Wilde after throwing a left hook and he hurt Wilde just before the bell with a rapid four-punch combination to the body. Benny Williams jumped into the ring at the bell to escort the tottering Wilde back to his corner.

At the start of the seventh, Villa walked through a feeble left from Wilde and drove him back on to the ropes with a left hook. Wilde covered up, but Pancho threw punches from every angle, landing anywhere he could. Wilde swayed left and right, trying desperately to avoid the avalanche of blows which came his way.

After what seemed like an eternity, Wilde managed to get off the ropes. Villa took a few steps back. Wilde followed him. Villa threw a left hook that landed flush on Jimmy's chin and then followed up with a devastating right. Wilde's whole body stiffened before he fell face first to the canvas. Referee Haley did not bother to count. As Wilde lay motionless, his cornermen

111 *Boxing* 27 June 1923

rushed through the ropes and unceremoniously picked him up and carried him back to his corner.

While Joe Humphreys announced the result to the dwindling crowd, an unconscious Wilde was carried to his dressing room. Elizabeth was distraught and on the verge of hysteria. Benny Williams lay Jimmy on a table and rubbed bags of ice on the top of his head and on the back of his neck.

The crowds of people who were filtering out of the Polo Grounds and into the warm night air were in a sombre mood. Many feared that Jimmy would not make it and were fully expecting to hear the news when they woke the following morning that he had died.

The greatest night of Pancho Villa's life had now become one of grave concern. Eventually, he managed to get into Wilde's dressing room.

'You – his wife?' Pancho asked Elizabeth in broken English.

Elizabeth nodded.

Pancho looked at Jimmy. Tears were gently running down Villa's face.

'Me no want to hurt him. Me not do that.'

With that, someone put their hand on the inconsolable Pancho's shoulder and quietly led him out of the room.

Very slowly, Jimmy started to come round. Movement came back to his eyes and limbs. Four hours after he had been knocked out, the physician from the New York State Athletic Commission reassured everyone in Wilde's dressing room that he would be okay to return to his quarters.

Jimmy and Elizabeth were besieged by newspaper reporters when they arrived at their apartment in Jersey City. Jimmy's pal, the bantamweight fighter Frankie Burns, and his wife, whisked Jimmy and Elizabeth off to their bungalow on Staten Island so that Jimmy could recuperate in peace.

Jimmy was in such a bad way that for three weeks, he lapsed in and out of consciousness. He was unable to eat solid foods and Elizabeth had to spoonfeed him ice cream. Slowly his faculties returned, but he could not remember anything about the fight after the blow that had felled him at the end of the second round.

Wilde's share of the gate, which amounted to $36,000 (equivalent to almost £380,000 in 2024) had nearly cost him his life.

21

Boxing Celebrity. Boxing Legend

WHEN WILDE returned home he was not able to do much. He was still in a bad way. Although his bruises healed, for some months after his fight with Villa he suffered from a constant headache and his memory had been affected. 'My mind was often a complete blank,' he would later write. 'I could hardly remember what I had said from one sentence to the next.'[112]

Wilde decided to seek advice from his friend Sir Alfred Fripp, the eminent surgeon to King George V, at his private practice in Marylebone.

Fripp strongly suspected that Jimmy had severe bruising on the brain and made it clear to him that he must never box again. One more blow to the head could cause a potentially fatal blood clot. Fripp reassured Jimmy that, by being careful, and with time, the headaches would stop. The debilitating headaches did eventually stop, but Wilde suffered from long- and short-term memory problems for the rest of his life.

112 Jimmy Wilde *Fighting Was My Business* p.255

Jimmy adapted well to retirement. Every day he would play at least one round of golf. When he was not at home with Elizabeth, he could be found at the racecourse with his friend, the champion flat jockey Steve Donoghue.

Two sad events defined 1925 for Wilde. At the end of January, 'Peerless' Jim Driscoll, arguably Britain's greatest-ever featherweight, as well as being Jimmy's cornerman and close friend, died from pneumonia at the age of 44. It is estimated that more than 100,000 people lined the streets to pay their respects as Driscoll's coffin was taken to the cemetery in Cardiff. Wilde said of Driscoll: 'He was the most conscientious fighter I ever knew in training. He would cover seven miles every morning, abstain completely from tobacco and drink, and go to bed before 10pm.'[113]

The second sad event was the death of Pancho Villa on 14 July in San Francisco. Villa, who was just 23, died of blood poisoning and Ludwig's angina, which had initially been caused by an infected tooth.

Unlike most fighters, Wilde retired from the ring a wealthy man. While David and Verdun were educated at King's College in Taunton, Jimmy and Elizabeth divided their time between their home in Radyr and their flat – which Jimmy had named 'Lonsdale' – in Cricklewood, north London.

With his friend Bill Collis, Wilde opened a betting shop in Cardiff and a cinema in Tylorstown. Both ventures provided a steady income.

It was through his dealings with theatre proprietor and financier James White that Wilde got his fingers burnt for the

113 Harry Carpenter *Masters Of Boxing* p.45

one and only time. White, who had dabbled in boxing promotion during the war, persuaded Wilde to invest in his upcoming production of *Katja The Dancer.*

Elizabeth was wary of White from the beginning and warned Jimmy to be careful. White assured Wilde that *Katja* was going to be a huge success. In all, Wilde gave White £10,000 to invest in the project. It was only when Wilde saw no return on his investment that the arguments between him and Elizabeth started.

Finally, Elizabeth had had enough. She was determined that Jimmy was not going to lend White any more money. To call White's bluff, she told Jimmy to visit White, tell him the betting shop was struggling and ask him for £1,000 up front. Jimmy called at White's office. He was unable to see him. For six days running, Wilde was fobbed off with excuses. White was either in a meeting or was away at a conference. Finally, on the seventh day, Wilde managed to see White, who promptly wrote Wilde a cheque and told him: 'You've got nothing to worry about Jim, there's a fortune in *Katja*. You'll be sitting absolutely pretty. Don't worry.'[114]

Wilde returned home and gave the cheque to Elizabeth, telling her not to worry and that White would come good, that he just needed a little more time.

Two months passed. There was no sign that the production had got under way and White had not been in touch. Then, on 1 July 1927, Wilde found out that White had taken his own life by swallowing hydrogen cyanide.

114 Jimmy Wilde *Fighting Was My Business* p.259

Losing £10,000 was a big blow. Wilde, however, was not the only person who had been swindled out of cash by White. The only thing he could do was put it down to experience.

At the beginning of the 1930s, Wilde sold his betting shop and the cinema. He had decided to spend his time training his son David, who, after a short amateur career, had made the decision to turn professional.

David Wilde made his professional debut in 1932 with a four-round points win over Joe Moore in Glasgow. Fighting as a featherweight, David compiled a 7-3-1 record. His wins were against fighters who had lost more than they had won and his three defeats were against men who had won more than they had lost. In 1934, David had his last fight and opened a barbershop in Edgware.

As is the case with most great sportsmen, Jimmy found coaching a frustrating experience. He struggled to understand why David had to work so hard to master something that had come so naturally to him. Nevertheless, Jimmy wanted to stay in the game he loved in some capacity. He applied to the southern area council of the British Boxing Board of Control for a referee's licence and went on to referee many fights in small halls over the next few years.

In 1933, Jimmy's former manager, Teddy Lewis, died at the age of 70 after suffering a seizure. Jimmy spoke fondly of the man who had looked after his interests throughout his illustrious career. 'A good manager, that is where the boys go wrong nowadays, see. They win a fight or two, success goes to their heads, somebody whispers in their ear that their manager is swindling them, and that is that. There are tons of clever people ready to give you advice. They kept telling me that my manager was doing me over. "Let him" I used to say to them. As long as I get my share, he can have his. I stuck with my manager. He was a good one.'[115]

Wilde was particularly keen on protecting young, up-and-coming fighters. With the help of his friend Dick Beech, Wilde set up the National Boxers Union in 1935. The NBU soon had more than 500 members and Jimmy, in his role as chairman, never hid the fact that the NBU had been set up to protect young boxers from being exploited by unscrupulous managers. While refereeing fights all over the country, Jimmy tried to sign up as many fighters as he could, but the managers held sway over the fighters to such a degree that subscriptions started to dwindle and the body quietly faded into obscurity.

Over the next decade, Wilde remained a hugely popular figure. He hosted quiz nights at rotary clubs, signed autographs, presented trophies at amateur boxing shows and worked as a second in the corners of professional fighters such as Herbie Smith from Gloucester and George Gale from Peterborough.

During the Second World War, Wilde travelled around Britain's dockyards urging dockers to invest in War Savings Certificates, telling them: 'You're pocket is your best pal. We've got the enemy punch drunk. Now we need your money to knock him out!'[116]

Wilde also gained immense satisfaction from raising money for hospitals, children's charities and boys' clubs during the war. He was always out with Elizabeth at some fundraising event or sportsman's dinner, where he would sign autographs and show off

115 *Western Mail* 18 April 1933
116 *Liverpool Echo* 11 February 1944

his Lonsdale belt to his admiring fans. Whenever he was asked who had hit him the hardest during his career, Jimmy would always reply with a deadpan face, 'My old woman, see, when I was late home,' before breaking into a smile and saying: 'No. Seriously, Pete Herman hit me the hardest.'

It was his long role as a boxing columnist for the *News of the World* and the *Empire News* though that enabled Wilde to really keep in touch with the fight game. Wilde would preview every big fight and then review it the following week. He was at ringside for all the major fights that took place at Harringay, Earl's Court, Olympia and White City from the mid-1930s until the early 50s.

Jimmy was always balanced and fair in his assessment of fights and fighters. He particularly liked skilful boxers who possessed a good left jab, Len Harvey for instance, as opposed to sluggers such as Freddie Mills, although Jimmy greatly admired Mills's heart and courage.

Jimmy, however, was never afraid to criticise when he felt it was justified. He did not think much of the Welsh flyweight Dai Dower and he bemoaned the number of soft European imports who would often come over and fold in the first round. When Randolph Turpin knocked out the Dutchman Luc van Dam in 48 seconds to win the European middleweight title in 1951, Jimmy wrote that 'a champion shouldn't be knocked out in the first round. He is supposed to have a fighting brain and instinct.'[117]

This was no slight on Turpin. Wilde, quite rightly, considered Turpin to be the best post-war British boxer of that era. In 1953, when Turpin purchased the Great Orme holiday resort in

117 *Empire News* 28 January 1951

Llandudno, Jimmy cut the ribbon to officially open 'Randy's Bar'. After that opening ceremony at the Great Orme, Wilde slowly faded from public life. He was diagnosed with diabetes – which he never managed very well – and began to spend more and more time at home in Cadoxton (near Barry in south Wales) with Elizabeth.

Wilde was still plagued by memory problems and headaches, which were no doubt further aggravated when he had a serious car accident in the spring of 1957. Wilde was travelling along the A4055 from Dinas Powys to Cadoxton when his car overturned. No other cars were involved, but Jimmy suffered bruising and severe concussion and spent two weeks in hospital.

A bout of appendicitis two years later hospitalised the champ again, this time for five weeks. While he was in hospital he was inducted into *The Ring* magazine's hall of fame, which was set up by its founder and editor Nat Fleischer. Most Americans knew Wilde as 'the ghost with a hammer in his hands'. When a reporter informed him that he had become the first non-American to be inducted, a weakened Wilde told the reporter: 'It's all I can do to lift a hammer these days.'[118]

Elizabeth told the *Western Mail* of Jimmy's health problems and the fact that in recent years he had felt increasingly lonely. 'Only a few people have been to see him,' she told the reporter. 'It's possible that they didn't know he was in hospital, but it's very strange, particularly when you think how popular he was. When I think back 40 years, nothing happened in London without Jimmy being invited. Now he's only got me.'[119]

118 Harry Carpenter *Masters Of Boxing* p.30
119 *Western Mail* 4 December 1959

Sadly, things did not get better. In March 1960, just three months after coming out of hospital, Jimmy was asked to present some cups and trophies at a local club in Cardiff. While waiting for his train home at Queen Street station, Jimmy was confronted by a man who headbutted him in the face and sent him tumbling backwards on to some luggage trolleys. Somebody found Jimmy lying semi-conscious on the platform some time later. He was taken to hospital where he had stitches on his cut nose. It was a totally unprovoked attack on a vulnerable 67-year-old.

For some reason, the story of Jimmy being attacked at the train station has been inaccurately documented over the years. Writers have always stated that Jimmy was attacked by a gang of feral youths in 1965. In fact, Wilde was actually attacked by a 40-year-old roof tiler named Trevor Dow, who lived in Trethomas. In August 1960, Dow, who had a history of violence, was found guilty of assaulting Wilde and sentenced to three years on probation.

Jimmy had been expected to give evidence at Cardiff law courts. When he did not show up, the police contacted Elizabeth, who assured them that he had left the house earlier that morning to make his way there. Cardiff police put out a search for him. Wilde eventually arrived at the court an hour after the case had been heard. Elizabeth apologised on Jimmy's behalf. 'He has a poor memory and probably forgot his destination,' she told reporters. 'He is meant to take insulin injections for his diabetes but has not done so this morning.'[120]

120 *Birmingham Post* 11 August 1960

In 1963, Jimmy had one last moment in the spotlight. The *Daily Mirror* ran a postal competition asking readers to vote for who they thought was the best British boxer to ever hold a Lonsdale belt. Wilde won by a landslide with 1,331 votes. The runner-up was Randy Turpin with a mere 267 votes.

The *Mirror*'s Sam Leitch visited Jimmy at his home in Barry to tell him the news. Jimmy told Leitch that he still watched the boxing on television. 'I would have earned half a million today,' he told Leitch wistfully. 'Instead, I fought 17 men a night for a kipper! But it's nice to be remembered.'[121]

Over the next 18 months, Jimmy's memory deteriorated rapidly. For a short time, Elizabeth's sister, Sarah, looked after him, but his condition worsened to such an extent that, in 1965, he was admitted to Whitchurch psychiatric hospital in Cardiff.

On 19 May 1965, Elizabeth passed away at the age of 71. By this time, Jimmy's dementia had progressed to such a stage that he did not know who Elizabeth was, let alone the fact that she had died.

Jimmy spent the last four years of his life at Whitchurch hospital. The nurses there loved him. They could not believe that the little old man sitting in front of them, who spent his days quietly staring into space, had once been the world's greatest boxer.

On 10 March 1969, Jimmy peacefully passed away. He was 76. Three days later, hundreds of mourners attended his funeral service at St Mary's Church in Barry, where he was laid to rest next to his beloved wife.

121 *Sunday Mirror* 17 February 1963

By the time Wilde died, many of the people who had been part of his story had also passed away. Perhaps this is why his passing was only fleetingly acknowledged in newspapers. Most, if not all, of those who had seen him in his prime were no longer around to provide reporters with anecdotes or first-hand accounts of his career.

In March 1975, *The Ring* magazine published its all-time division-by-division rankings. Wilde sat at the top of the flyweight division. His old foe Pancho Villa was at number two. The man who Wilde should have fought, Frankie Genaro, was rated at number three.

Fifteen years later, in June 1990, Wilde was among the first batch of fighters to be inducted into the International Boxing Hall of Fame in Canastota, New York. Wilde took his place alongside such ring legends as Jack Dempsey, Jack Johnson, Benny Leonard, Henry Armstrong, Willie Pep, Sugar Ray Robinson and Muhammad Ali.

In March 1994, *The Ring* named Wilde as the greatest-ever Welsh boxer in its 'Best of a Nation' feature. Wilde, sadly, had largely been forgotten in Britain, but his legend lived on in America. Two months later, when *The Ring* revised its division-by-division rankings, Wilde was still considered to be the greatest flyweight of all time. The fantastic Mexican from the 1970s, Miguel Canto, was at number two, with Argentine legend Pascual Perez at number three.

A century after his last fight, Jimmy Wilde is still the man all other world flyweight champions are measured against.

Jimmy Wilde's Fight Record

1911

Mar 20	Dai Thomas	W	KO	3	Pontypridd
May 8	Jim Easton	W	PTS	15	Edinburgh
May 29	Billy Bowen	W	KO	4	Pontypridd
Aug 29	Young Jennings	W	KO	11	Pontypridd

1912

Jan 20	Matt Wells Nipper	W	KO	1	London
Feb 1	Young Baker	W	PTS	6	Liverpool
Jul 20	Kid Morris	W	KO	5	Cardiff
Aug 12	Mike Flynn	W	PTS	8	Tonypandy
Aug 17	Jim Stuckey	W	KO	8	Tonypandy
Sep 19	Walter Hall	W	KO	3	Sheffield
Nov 9	Phil Davies	W	KO	2	Merthyr
Nov 16	Young Rainsford	W	KO	2	Tonypandy
Nov 23	Kid Pearson	W	KO	2	Mountain Ash
Nov 30	Alf Williams	W	PTS	12	Pentre
Dec 1	Stoker Staines	W	KO	1	Tonypandy
Dec 21	Billy Yates	W	KO	4	Cardiff

1913

Jan 1	Billy Padden	W	KO	18	Glasgow
Jan 18	Tommy Hughes	W	KO	7	Tonypandy
Feb 1	Dick Jenkins	W	ND	10	Tonypandy
Feb 15	Young Fitzpatrick	W	KO	3	Tonypandy
Mar 8	Dai Mathews	W	KO	4	Tonypandy
Mar 31	Harry Taylor	W	KO	3	Swansea
Apr 12	Will Rees	W	KO	2	Tonypandy
Apr 19	Billy Yates	W	KO	4	Tonypandy
May 24	Dai 'Chips' Davies	W	PTS	10	Tonypandy
Jun 14	Billy Padden	W	PTS	12	Tonypandy

Jun 21	Gwillym Thomas	W	KO	5	Tonypandy
Jul 1	Dick Lewis	W	KO	3	Tonypandy
Jul 12	Tommy Lewis	W	PTS	12	Tonypandy
Jul 19	George Dando	W	PTS	15	Tonypandy
Aug 4	Darkie Saunders	W	PTS	10	Cardiff
Aug 28	Jack Dyer	W	KO	3	Liverpool
Sep 8	Dido Gains	W	PTS	15	Cardiff
Sep 11	Harry Curley	W	KO	12	Hanley
Sep 18	Kid Levene	W	KO	7	Hanley
Sep 22	George Dando	W	PTS	20	Cardiff
Nov 1	Darkie Saunders	W	KO	11	Tonypandy
Nov 13	Young Baker	W	KO	10	Liverpool
Nov 21	Jack Dyer	W	KO	2	Manchester
Nov 22	Dido Gains	W	PTS	15	Swansea
Dec 6	George Dando	W	DQ	10	Merthyr
Dec 13	Billy Charles	W	KO	6	Tonypandy
Dec 15	Harry Brooke	W	KO	9	Manchester

1914

Jan 3	Albert Nutter	W	PTS	15	Tonypandy
Jan 8	Young Beynon	W	PTS	15	Liverpool
Jan 29	Billy Padden	W	KO	3	Liverpool
Feb 2	Albert Nutter	W	PTS	15	Birkenhead
Feb 9	Tom Thomas	W	KO	7	Manchester
Feb 12	Paddy Carroll	W	KO	2	Liverpool
Feb 16	George Jaggers	W	KO	5	Sheffield
Mar 26	Bill Kyne	W	KO	4	Liverpool
Mar 30	Eugene Husson	W	KO	6	London
Apr 13	Jack Madden	W	KO	4	Ashton-under-Lyne
Apr 16	Albert Bouzzonie	W	PTS	15	Liverpool
Apr 27	Alf Mansfield	W	PTS	20	Leeds
May 11	Georges Gloria	W	KO	9	London
Jun 22	Charlie Banyard	W	KO	9	Aberdare
Jul 18	Charlie Lorden	W	KO	11	Tonypandy
Jul 23	Artie Edwards	W	PTS	15	Liverpool
Aug 10	Young Walters	W	DQ	6	Newcastle
Aug 20	Young Baker	W	PTS	15	Leicester
Sep 28	Alf Mansfield	W	KO	10	London
Nov 16	Joe Symonds	W	PTS	15	London
Dec 3	Sid Smith	W	KO	9	Liverpool

1915

Jan 25	Tancy Lee	L	KO	17	London
(acant British flyweight title)					
May 25	Sid Shields	W	KO	2	Liverpool
Jul 24	Driver Benthew	W	KO		Carbrook
Aug 14	George Clark	W	KO	8	Carbrook
Sep 23	Walter Buchan	W	KO	5	Liverpool
Oct 20	Peter Cullen	W	KO	9	Dublin
Nov 27	Tommy Hughes	W	KO	8	Barrow
Dec 9	Johnny Best	W	KO	14	Liverpool
Dec 13	Danny Elliot	W	KO	2	Bradford
Dec 20	Sid Smith	W	KO	8	London

1916

Jan 8	Billy Rowlands	W	KO	7	Swansea
Jan 24	Tommy Noble	W	KO	11	London
Jan 27	Jim Morton	W	KO	2	Liverpool
Feb 14	Joe Symonds	W	KO	12	London
(British flyweight title)					
Mar 9	Sam Keller	W	KO	8	London
Mar 27	Sid Smith	W	KO	3	London
Apr 24	Johnny Rosner	W	KO	11	Liverpool
Apr 29	Benny Thomas	W	PTS	15	Cardiff
May 13	Darkie Saunders	W	KO	3	London
May 13	Young Magnus	W	KO	2	London
May 29	Tommy Harrison	W	KO	8	London
Jun 26	Tancy Lee	W	KO	11	London
(British flyweight title)					
Jul 31	Johnny Hughes	W	KO	10	London
(British flyweight title)					
Nov 9	Tommy Noble	W	KO	15	Liverpool
Dec 18	Young Zulu Kid	W	KO	11	London
(World flyweight title)					

1917

Mar 12	George Clark	W	KO	4	London
(British flyweight title)					
Mar 22	Jimmy Russell	W	KO	3	London

1918

Apr 29	Dick Heasman	W	KO	2	London
(British flyweight title)					
Aug 31	Joe Conn	W	KO	12	London

1919

Mar 31	Joe Lynch	W	PTS	15	London
Apr 21	Jimmy Buck	W	KO	5	Liverpool
May 16	Alf Mansfield	W	KO	13	London
Jul 17	Pal Moore	W	PTS	20	London
Dec 6	Jackie Sharkey		ND	10	Milwaukee

1920

Jan 8	Johnny Aher		ND	8	St Louis MO
Jan 29	Mike Ertle	W	KO	3	Milwaukee
Feb 19	Mickey Russell	W	KO	7	Jersey City
Mar 3	Patsy Wallace		ND	6	Philadelphia
Mar 12	Frankie Mason		ND	12	Toledo OH
Apr 12	Young Zulu Kid		ND	10	Windsor ON
Apr 21	Al Murray	W	KO	8	Camden NJ
May 1	Bobby Dyson	W	KO	1	Lawrence MA
May 13	Al Murray	W	KO	2	Philadelphia
May 24	Patsy Wallace		ND	10	Toronto

1921

Jan 13	Pete Herman	L	KO	17	London

1923

Jun 18	Pancho Villa	L	KO	7	New York City
(World flyweight title)					

FIGHTS	**WON**	**LOST**	**NO DECISION**
110 (78 KO)	100	3	7

Jimmy Wilde's Tale of the Tape

HEIGHT

5ft 2½in

WEIGHT

6st 10lb

REACH

66in

WAIST

26in

CHEST

31½in

THIGH

21in

WRIST

6in

FIST

9in

BICEP

11½in

BIBLIOGRAPHY

Andre, Sam and Fleischer, Nat *A Pictorial History of Boxing* Hamlyn, London, 1978

Bell, Leslie *Bella of Blackfriars* Odhams Press, London, 1961

Carpenter, Harry *Masters of Boxing* Heinmann, London, 1964

Deghy, Guy *Noble and Manly: The History of The National Sporting Club* Hutchinson, London, 1956

Fleischer, Nat *The Ring Record Book & Boxing Encyclopaedia* The Ring Bookshop, New York, 1972

Golesworthy, Maurice *Encyclopaedia of Boxing* Hale, London, 1975

Harding, John *Lonsdale's Belt: The Story of Boxing's Greatest Prize* Robson, London, 1994

Heller, Peter *In This Corner…! Forty World Champions Tell Their Stories* Robson, London, 1985

Muulan, Harry *The Illustrated History of Boxing* Hamlyn, London, 1987

Roberts, James B & Skutt, Alexander G *The Boxing Register* McBooks Press, USA, 2011

Sugar, Bert Randolph *Boxing's 100 Greatest Fighters* Hale, London, 2006

Wilde, Jimmy *Fighting Was My Business* Joseph, London, 1938

Wilde, Jimmy *The Art of Boxing* Webster's, London, 1923

Newspapers

Birmingham Post, Cambrian Daily Leader, Daily Herald, Daily Mirror, Daily Record Glasgow, Dublin Evening Telegraph, Leeds

Mercury, Liverpool Echo, Manchester Sporting Chronicle, Mirror of Life, News of the World, North Western Daily Mail, Plymouth Herald, Porthcawl News, Scottish Referee, Sheffield Daily Telegraph, Sheffield Independent, South Wales Weekly Post, Sports Argus, Sporting Life, Staffordshire Sentinel, The Scotsman, Glasgow Herald, The Globe, The Sportsman, Weekly Dispatch, Western Daily Press, Western Mail.

Magazines

Boxing

The Ring

Websites

boxrec.com

boxinghistory.org.uk

britishnewspaperarchive.co.uk